Costume Jewellery

A Collector's Guide

Caroline Behr

Special Consultant:
Tracy Tolkien

MILLER'S COSTUME JEWELLERY: A COLLECTOR'S GUIDE
by Caroline Behr
Special Consultant: Tracy Tolkien

First published in Great Britain in 2001 by Miller's, a
Mitchell Beazley, imprints of Octopus Publishing Gro
2–4 Heron Quays, London E14 4JP

Miller's is a registered trademark of Octopus Publish
Copyright © Octopus Publishing Group Ltd 2001
Reprinted 2002, 2004

Commissioning Editor **Anna Sanderson**
Executive Art Editor **Rhonda Fisher**
Designer **Louise Griffiths**
Project Editor **Emily Anderson**
Editor **Catherine Blake**
Proofreader **Joan Porter**
Indexer **Sue Farr**
Picture Research **Jenny Faithful, Nick Wheldon**
Production **Nancy Roberts, Deborah Wehner**
Jacket photography by **Stuart Chorley**

The publishers will be grateful for any information that will assist them
in keeping future editions up to date. Although all reasonable care
has been taken in the preparation of this book, neither the publishers
nor the compilers can accept any liability for any consequence arising
from the use thereof, or the information contained therein.

ISBN 1 84000 373 1
A CIP record for this book is available from the British Library

To order this book as a gift or incentive contact
Mitchell Beazley on 020 7531 8481

Please note that unfortunately it is not possible for Miller's Publications
to provide valuations for any personal items

Set in Bembo, Frutiger, and Shannon
Produced by Toppan Printing Co., (HK) Ltd.
Printed and bound in China

Jacket illustrations, from top to bottom: Miriam Haskell faux
pearl necklace, 1950s, **£150–250/$225–375**; paste bracelet,
1930s, **£200–300/$300–450**; silver gilt butterfly by Rya, 1940s,
£175–275/$275–400; earrings by Jomaz, 1950s, **£50–75/$75–100**;
pink glass earrings, 1950s, unsigned, **£35–50/$55–75**
Half-title page: Pierrot head brooch with Swarovski crystals, c.1995,
w. 5.5cm/2¼in, **£70–90/$105–135**; **Contents page:** Boucher seated
poodle, 1950s, ht 5cm/2in, **£30–50/$45–75**

ie
ry

Guide

THE LONDON BOROUGH
www.bromley.gov.uk

Please return/renew this item
by the last date shown.
Books may also be renewed by
phone and Internet.

Bromley Libraries

30128 80008 441 3

contents

Introduction

Costume jewellery is an exciting and fast-growing collecting area. Broadly defined as jewellery made from non-precious materials, its appeal is in the original design, skilful use of colour, high standards of craftsmanship and sometimes sheer spirit of fantasy. Many pieces of costume jewellery are, in a modest way, a part of social history. More light-heartedly, they often provide reasonably priced fashion accessories, and sometimes even a successful financial investment, although, as in many other collecting areas, the rule should be to buy for pleasure rather than making a profit.

The fun and excitement of collecting costume jewellery lies in its variety. The new collector should take the time to learn the facts and educate the eye. The best way to start is to spend time looking at the jewellery: visit specialist shops and dealers, handle the pieces, weigh them in your hand, and ask questions. Most dealers have chosen to specialize because they love costume jewellery and will enjoy sharing their enthusiasm. Dealers know that collecting starts from admiration for a piece, so an enthusiast is a collector in the

Paste flip-top watch, 1950s, l. 18cm/7in, £130–160/$195–240

making. Reference books and sales and exhibition catalogues (see p.61) are also valuable ways of learning, and new ones are appearing all the time. Some major museums already have sections devoted to costume jewellery, and these are likely to be expanded as interest continues to grow.

What should you buy? There are many ways of collecting costume jewellery. Some collectors like to form wide-ranging, wearable collections of reasonably priced items geared to their wardrobes and style preferences, while others prefer to concentrate their resources on a few spectacular showpieces, or a particular period or maker. Some collectors like to piece together the elaborate parures of the 1950s and '60s: by acquiring a matching necklace, brooch, earrings and bracelet, you will add greatly to the interest, not to mention the value, of each individual piece. You might focus on a theme, such as baskets, bows or insects. For example, one recent collector took as her starting point the lizard, or salamander, used in jewellery from the Middle Ages as an emblem of passionate love, due to its ability to thrive in fire. In costume jewellery of the late 19thC the lizard was encapsulated in marcasite and diamanté, in the 1940s it was used by the American manufacturer Coro as a striking example of cocktail jewellery, and in the 1980s it was reinterpreted by the English costume jewellers Butler & Wilson, and worn to great effect by the late Diana, Princess of Wales.

Orange blossom brooch by Iradj Moini, 1990s, l. 10.5cm/4¼in, £300–500/$450–750

Where should you buy? Junk shops, charity shops, car boot sales, dress agencies and vintage clothes shops are all good sources. In a higher price range, specialist dealers and auction houses offer reliable expertise for the novice collector, and are often the best sources overall for rare, important pieces. If a question of authenticity arises, you can return your purchase and expect a full refund. Wherever you buy period costume jewellery, always ask for a receipt giving an approximate date, and if applicable, the designer of each piece. If you want to resell, the same dealer or auction house can advise if prices have increased. Taking photographs, even simple Polaroids, of your purchases also provides a useful record.

The Internet has added a new dimension to buying and selling costume jewellery, widening the scope of what is available worldwide to every collector. It is not possible to examine such details as makers' marks on a website, but if you know exactly what piece you are looking for, it can save much time and effort. Using a credit card to pay will protect you if the item is faulty or is never delivered.

Once you have started to acquire pieces of costume jewellery, wearing them is, of course, one of the great pleasures of ownership. However, to maintain the value and condition of your pieces a few basic rules should be observed (see p.60, Care and Repair).

As we enter the 21stC some of the best costume jewellery of the 1980s and 1990s is already considered collectable. Many new exhibitions are being planned and collector's clubs are thiving. In this positive climate it seems certain that costume jewellery will remain a popular collecting field in the foreseeable future, continuing to give pleasure through its style, accessibility and ability to express the spirit of an era.

Lizard diamanté brooch by Butler & Wilson, 2001 reproduction of a 1980s design, l. 20cm/8in, **£150–175/$225–265**

Prices & dimensions

Prices vary depending on the condition of the piece, its rarity and where it is purchased, so the prices given are an approximate guide only. The sterling/dollar conversion has been made at a rate of £1 = $1.50 (adjust the dollar value as necessary to accord with current exchange rates). Measurements of width or length are given to the nearest half centimetre/quarter inch.

Victorian

During Queen Victoria's reign (1837–1901) jewellery became accessible to all for the first time. The Victorian genius for invention led to the discovery of new materials, while old ones were made more readily available. Improved means of mass-production transformed these materials into attractive jewels, purchased by an increasingly affluent middle class. The Queen herself influenced the styles of the day. Aside from her love of grand court jewels, studded with gemstones, she also had more modest tastes, reflected in the narrow enamel band she always wore (a secret betrothal ring from Prince Albert), the mourning jewellery introduced after his death, and the lockets, cameos and commemorative pieces she gave to her family and household. These pieces are increasingly popular today.

◄ **Jet necklace**
Jet is fossilized pine, similar to a hard coal or anthracite, found in large deposits near Whitby in Yorkshire. It became the height of fashion for mourning jewellery when it was worn by Queen Victoria after the death of Prince Albert in 1861. The more highly carved the necklace, the more valuable it usually is; the deep lustrous colouring, detailed hand-carving and good condition make this a highly desirable piece. Matching earrings or a bracelet would increase its value.

Jet necklace,
1860–90,
l. 50cm/19¾in,
£350–400/
$525–600

▼ **Jet brooch**
This is a typical oval brooch, with fine carving of leaf and ropework borders and central abstract motif. It is mounted on the back with a small ring, allowing it to be worn as a pendant. The most desirable jet brooches are those with a locket compartment set in the reverse, used for carrying a lock of hair or a small photograph of a departed loved one. In 1887, the year of her Golden Jubilee, Queen Victoria relaxed the strict court etiquette for mourning; ladies returned to lighter clothes and jewels, and the heyday of jet was over, although it continued to be made until the 1920s.

Jet brooch,
1860–90,
l. 5.5cm/2¼in,
£250–300/
$375–450

Value & condition
• Victorian jewellery has recovered its popularity, and good examples now hold or increase in value.
• The new collector should look for an attractive design in reasonable condition.
• A good-quality piece may still have repairs or restoration: a specialist dealer will advise.

Vulcanite cameo brooch, late 19thC, l. 5.5cm/2¼in, **£120–150/$180–225**

▲ Vulcanite cameo brooch

In imitation of jet, this brooch is made out of an early material called vulcanite. A scientist, Charles Goodyear, developed vulcanite by hardening, or vulcanizing, rubber by heating it with sulphur. Moulded rather than carved, it is less expensive than real jet but is nevertheless a collector's category in its own right. Here it has been used to make a cameo brooch, one of the most popular of all Victorian jewels. The pattern is a later Victorian style, featuring a romanticized female head.

▼ Beadwork cuff bracelet

One of the accomplishments of a Victorian young lady, the craft of beadwork was well-established in Britain and Europe from the 17thC. It follows the fashions of embroidery but because its raw materials, usually glass beads, are more durable, many pieces survive today in mint condition. A bracelet such as this one below, with its typical sentimental decoration of roses, is pretty, colourful and highly collectable, and sometimes comes in matched pairs. Beadwork belts and bags are also popular. Condition of these pieces is particularly important, as restoration of beadwork is difficult and costly.

Beadwork cuff bracelet, c.1890, w. 8.5cm/3½in, **£150–200/$225–300**

Italian mosaic brooch, c.1900, w. 5cm/2in, **£60–70/$90–105**

▲ Italian glass mosaic brooch

Victorian glass mosaic jewellery, from the grandest pieces to the most humble, is a popular and collectable category. This example is one of numerous "souvenir" items made in Italy for the ever-growing tourist trade, and is inspired by the classical art of mosaic jewellery, revived in the 19thC by such jewellers as Castellani of Rome. Condition is very important as mosaic is a difficult technique to repair.

Pinchbeck

Pinchbeck is a gold substitute created from an alloy of zinc and copper. It was invented in about 1720 by Christopher Pinchbeck (1671–1732), a London watch and clockmaker, and originally used for watch cases. True pinchbeck was only made by Pinchbeck and his son until the 1830s, after which the term was used more generally to indicate quality gilt metal. Highly prized for its warm, burnished appearance and lightness, it has always been popular with jewellery lovers, and is increasingly sought after by costume jewellery collectors. This versatile material was used for mesh jewellery and muff chains, and for items of high Victorian fashion, particularly brooches, in ingenious interpretations of real gold jewellery. A superb pinchbeck chatelaine (c.1760) was one of the highlights of the late Diana Vreeland's costume jewellery collection. Pinchbeck jewels are unmarked.

▼ Lion-head brooch
The reign of Queen Victoria (1837–1901) saw a wide range of styles in jewellery, interpreted in both precious and semi-precious materials. This magnificent brooch, with its lion's head motifs in Archaeological Revival style, would have been prohibitively expensive in gold. In pinchbeck, it was affordable and probably used to fasten an outside garment, such as the voluminous shawl fashionable at the time.

Pinchbeck lion-head brooch, 1860–80, w. 7cm/2¾in, **£200–250/ $300–375**

Pinchbeck buckle brooch, 1840–60, w. 5cm/2in, **£140–180/ $210–270**

◄ Buckle brooch
Belt buckles were made in a variety of metals, including pinchbeck, from the late 18thC onwards. During the Victorian era the belt buckle became a popular motif in jewellery, used on bracelets, brooches, pendants and lockets. On this piece, the matt, rich golden surface and raised design give the impression of weight, when it is in fact very light.

Pinchbeck tiaras

Pinchbeck can be admired in its most decorative form in the A. Beckett Terrell Collection of Empire Combs and Frontlets, at the Birmingham Museum & Art Gallery, in England. The collection contains over 100 pinchbeck tiaras, dating from 1820 to the 1840s. Most of them are set with high-quality paste stones.

▼ Flower brooch with safety chain

A delicate diamond flower on a blue background is a popular motif on 19thC jewellery, and here fine pinchbeck scrollwork has been used to frame a central forget-me-not of tiny diamond chips, on a ground of lapis lazuli or a pseudo lapis such as the mineral sodalite. The forget-me-not was a popular symbol of eternal love.

Pinchbeck flower brooch with safety chain, 1840–60, l. 4cm/1½in (excluding chain), **£150–200/$225–300**

"Pinchbeck" Art Nouveau insect brooch, c.1890, l. 7cm/2¾in, **£200–250/$300–375**

▲ "Pinchbeck" Art Nouveau insect brooch

The term "pinchbeck" is often erroneously used to describe a variety of base metals. This brooch is more likely to be "tombac", one of a number of metal alloys made in France from the late 18thC. It would appeal to a fan of Art Nouveau (see pp.16–17) because of its strong, authentic Art Nouveau design and reasonable price for this expensive area. The imitation emerald pendant is a later addition to the piece.

▼ Hair brooch

A locket containing a decorative motif made from human hair was a popular item of Victorian sentimental jewellery. These were often made by ladies at home in memory of a loved one, or to celebrate a betrothal or wedding. The reverse of this "swivel" brooch contains a sepia photograph.

Pinchbeck hair brooch, c.1850, w. 5cm/2in, **£100–120/$150–180**

Czech jewellery

The kingdom of Bohemia, now part of modern Czechoslovakia, has traditionally been famous for its glass-making, which included the manufacture of high-quality glass stones for costume jewellery. From the mid 19thC these were made in vast quantities and exported to the costume jewellery centres of Europe, such as Paris. The industry was based in Gablonz (now Jablonec), which developed its own modest costume jewellery industry: in 1880 a School for Applied Arts was founded, and specimens of jewellery were sent from Vienna for students to copy. Jewellery was also made by outworkers, who used locally produced glass stones and metal fittings supplied by middlemen. From the 1890s to the outbreak of World War II, a distinctive style of costume jewellery was produced, now popular with collectors. Czech jewellery is usually unsigned but occasionally it is marked "Czech" or "Czechoslovakia".

Imitation lapis and jade necklace, late 1920s/1930s, l. 37.5cm/ (14¾in), **£250–300/ $375–450**

◀ **Imitation lapis and jade necklace**
The style of this necklace is obviously influenced by Art Deco trends (see pp.20–21), but this is undercut by the imitation pearl and jade festoons, which are not at all Deco. Czech necklaces are rarer than brooches, and the more complex the metalwork and stones, the more desirable the piece. This one is highly collectable.

▼ **Butterfly brooch with turquoise glass stones**
Filigree backings are a characteristic of Czech brooches, giving them their delicate, lacy look. Figural subjects such as this butterfly are rare: Czech brooches are usually oval, round or square, though bows, flowers and stars are also found. These brooches are not enormously valuable but they are certainly collectable.

Butterfly brooch with turquoise-coloured glass stones, 1920s, w. 7.5cm/3in, **£70–90/ $105–135**

Multicolour brooch,
1920s, w. 7cm/3in,
£50–70/$75–105

▲ Multicolour brooch

This is a typical Czech brooch as they tend to be large (7–10cm/3–4in) and set with multicoloured pastes, although items that are all one colour can also be found. Czech pastes come in a wonderful range of colours, such as deep purple and cranberry, or the palest pinks, greens and yellows. During the 1930s these brooches tended to have larger stones.

▼ Imitation coral and amethyst necklace

The orange and purple colour combination of this collectable necklace is unusual, yet its mixture of glass stones and beads, here textured and ribbed, is typical. Enamel is also found in Czech pieces. Sometimes Czech components were used on plastic backings and assembled in France. However, this piece is signed "Czechoslovakia".

Imitation coral and amethyst necklace, 1930s, l. 37cm/14½in,
£140–160/$210–240

Czech bags
An increasingly collectable area of Czech jewellery is the handbag. The clasps show similar workmanship to brooches, and were probably exported to France where they were made into mesh or beadwork bags. Often mirrors are incorporated as well.

FACT FILE

Cuff bracelet with imitation turquoise and topaz, 1930s, w. 6.5cm/2½in,
£250–300/$375–450

▲ Cuff bracelet with imitation turquoise and topaz

Bracelets are some of the rarest Czech pieces, and this one is outstanding for its size, detail and quality of its pastes. The metalwork incorporates a decoration of leaves and lions' heads at each side of the clasp. The jewellery-makers of Gablonz interpreted most of the popular motifs of the period, including Egyptian Revival and Chinese designs.

Edwardian paste

The brief reign of Edward VII and his consort Queen Alexandra, known as the Edwardian era (1901–10), was a heyday of gracious, leisured living. Ladies and gentlemen of high society, enriched by the prosperity of the British Empire, dressed themselves in clothes and jewels that displayed their wealth and social status. In the daytime ladies dressed in light silks and gauzes, with large picture hats, and in the evening they wore elaborate lace gowns, set off by jewels in the "garland" style that had been introduced by the French jeweller Cartier in the 1890s. This delicate, nostalgic style of jewellery, usually made from diamonds and platinum and based on 18thC originals, was widely copied in its own time in a variety of materials, and is still popular with collectors of costume jewellery today.

Edwardian basket
necklace, c.1910,
l. 40cm/15¾in,
**£180–200/
$270–300**

▶ **Basket necklace**
This short necklace of paste stones set in silver incorporates two of the favourite sentimental motifs of the Edwardian era: a basket of flowers, and a linking ribbon bow. The touches of pale pink and green are characteristic of the period, as is pale mauve. This necklace might have originally come with matching or related pieces such as a brooch, pendant, bracelet or earrings. It is unsigned but its delicate pattern and fine workmanship suggest that it may be of French manufacture.

▼ **Crown brooch**
Crown brooches first appeared in the Victorian and Edwardian eras as a symbol of respect and affection for the monarchy and have since been a popular theme in costume jewellery. This piece is inspired by the Queen Consort's crown worn by Queen Alexandra at her coronation in 1902. Other brooches are of plain diamanté or fantasy style. Earlier crowns such as this are unsigned up until the 1940s.

Edwardian crown brooch,
1902, w. 3.5cm/1¼in, **£80–90/
$120–135**

▼ Edwardian earrings

Pairs of earrings are a popular collecting area in Edwardian paste jewellery and are rarer than other pieces as one of a pair can be easily lost. Examples of the period are usually pendant, as opposed to button type, designed to be worn with the elaborate upswept coiffures of the time. They can be either screw-back, as here, or for pierced ears. Being long and elaborate in shape, this pair is particularly collectable; the silver setting has a characteristic "chunky" quality, which is part of its appeal.

Pair of Edwardian earrings, c.1902, l. 9cm/3½in, **£360–380/$540–570**

Edwardian lizard brooch, c.1910, l. 7cm/2¾in, **£180–200/$270–300**

▲ Lizard brooch

This is Edwardian paste jewellery in more playful mood: a brooch in a lizard/salamander motif, also found in Victorian jewellery and successfully revived by Butler & Wilson in the 1980s. Lizards appear in a variety of sinuous poses, in paste, marcasite and real diamonds, often with a series of green or pink stones along the back. This piece has been skilfully restored with later high-quality paste stones. If one of the original paste stones is missing, restorers often prefer to replace them all, to ensure an even match of material and colour. Other common Edwardian animal motifs include monkeys, elephants and tigers.

▼ Marcasite brooch

This brooch, with its typical central motif of a vase of flowers, is made of marcasite, a naturally shiny metallic substance of a gunmetal grey, cut from the mineral iron pyrites. During the 18th and 19thC, marcasite was popular as a diamond substitute all over Europe, especially in Switzerland, where sumptuary laws governing the lavishness of dress according to rank restricted the wearing of diamonds.

Edwardian marcasite brooch, c.1910, diam. 5cm/2in, **£80–100/$120–150**

Art Nouveau

The sinuous forms of Art Nouveau began to appear in most areas of the decorative arts from the early 1880s, and it soon became an international movement. Partly inspired by art and literature, partly by love of nature and Japanese art, it was also a reaction against the conventional forms of the mid 19thC. In the United States the style was known as "Tiffany" as it was developed by the leading jeweller Tiffany & Co., in Germany as "Jugendstil" ("Youth style") and in Italy "Stile Liberty", after Arthur L. Liberty's shop in Regent Street, London. (Liberty was the leading British retailer of the style.) The impact of Art Nouveau jewellery came from the originality of the design and quality of the workmanship, rather than expensive gold and gemstones. Nevertheless, pieces by well-known makers, such as the ones on these pages, now command very high prices and a new collector is advised to look for Art Nouveau designs on unsigned pieces by small jewellers.

Fantasy fish
pendant,
c.1900,
l. 6.5cm/2½in,
**£1,000–2,000/
$1,500–3,000**

▼ Fantasy fish pendant

This gilded silver, garnet and chalcedony (quartz and crystal) pendant, signed "ES", is by Eduard Schöpflich, a well-known Munich-based jeweller of the turn of the century. The motif of a writhing, asymmetrical fantasy fish is typically Art Nouveau, and similar to other popular motifs of a griffin or chimera. The use of polished cabochon (domed) stones is also typical: semi-precious stones are shown to their best advantage when polished rather than faceted, and the effect is more in keeping with the Art Nouveau naturalist ideal.

▶ Gilded silver & garnet ring

The characteristic swirling, rounded lines of Art Nouveau forms lent themselves perfectly to the curved shape of a ring, here engraved with the typical image of a female face with flowing hair. In the USA the design was known as "Flor-a-Dora", after a popular musical comedy. The ideal of a free feminine spirit owes much to the influence of Pre-Raphaelite paintings and to growing female emancipation. The ring bears no maker's mark but the style suggests European manufacture.

Gilded silver
and garnet
ring, c.1900,
w. 2.5cm/1in,
**£1,000–2,000/
$1,500–3,000**

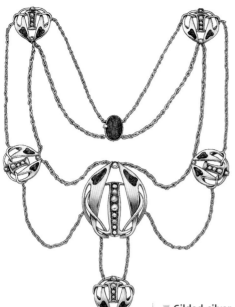

Tiffany & Co.

America's leading jeweller made Art Nouveau pieces from the 1880s. At the 1889 Exposition Universelle Tiffany established its reputation internationally with chief designer Paulding Farnham's 25 spectacular orchid brooches, now considered some of the finest examples of early Art Nouveau.

FACT FILE

Liberty & Co. gold necklace, c.1900, l. 8cm/3in (pendant only), **£10,000–12,000/$15,000–18,000**

▲ Liberty & Co. necklace

The firm of Liberty & Co., with its shop in Regent Street, London, was the most important retailer of Art Nouveau in Britain. Arthur Lasenby Liberty commissioned designs from some of the leading jewellers of the time, including Archibald Knox (1864–1933) from the Isle of Man – an enthusiast of the Celtic Revival movement. This outstanding gold Liberty necklace displays all the features associated with Knox's Art Nouveau style: flowing lines, intertwined shapes and turquoise enamel highlights.

▼ Gilded silver, amethyst & opal belt buckle

Belt buckles were a popular item of Art Nouveau jewellery: those designed by Archibald Knox for Liberty are a collector's category in their own right. This buckle by the Paris firm of René Beauclair bears the typical flowing and seductive lines of French Art Nouveau.

Gilded silver belt buckle by René Beauclair, c.1900, w. 8cm/3in, **£3,000–5,000/$4,500–7,500**

Enamel bee brooch by Meyle and Mayer, c.1900, w. 5cm/2in, **£1,000–2,000/$1,500–3,000**

▲ Enamel bee brooch

This enamel bee is by Meyle and Mayer, a German company based in Pforzheim that made a range of Art Nouveau jewellery, and bears their mark of a dragonfly.

The wings are of typical *plique-à-jour* enamel: translucent enamel with no backing in a metal framework, producing an effect of delicacy and lightness.

Arts & Crafts

The Arts and Crafts movement, led by the British writer and art critic John Ruskin (1819–1900) and his kindred spirit William Morris, began as a reaction to the machine age. They and others urged a return to pre-industrial levels of craftsmanship, looking back to the Middle Ages for inspiration. Architects and craftsmen in Britain and elsewhere followed their lead. Many of them produced superb one-off pieces for wealthy patrons, some of whom misunderstood their high ideals. (The leading Arts and Crafts jeweller Henry Wilson made an elaborate tiara for Lady Llewellyn Smith with a central figure of Orpheus subduing the wild beasts with his harp; she was embarrassed by the nudity of the musician and asked for a detachable loin-cloth to be made for it.) The movement's socialist principles encouraged its followers to explore the potential of less costly materials and simple designs.

Silver and bowenite brooch by Edgar Simpson, c.1900, l. 4cm/1½in, **£1,000–2,000/$1,500–3,000**

▶ **Silver & bowenite brooch**
Nottingham jeweller Edgar Simpson produced a range of Arts and Crafts jewels, mostly in the Celtic Revival style. This brooch, marked "ES", features tree-of-life and ropework decoration on silver, set with bowenite – a jade-like mineral used for inlay work since ancient times. Simpson's work was admired by Charles Rennie Mackintosh, the most influential architect and designer of his day, and was exhibited at the landmark Vienna Sezession exhibition of 1900.

▼ **Silver & enamel brooch**
Frances McNair was one of the influential "Glasgow Four" group who also comprised Charles Rennie Mackintosh, his wife Margaret and Frances' husband Herbert McNair. Their metalwork and jewellery shows the same commitment to the Celtic Revival style. It was widely exhibited and spread the ideals of the Arts and Crafts movement in Europe.

Gilded silver and enamel brooch by Frances McNair, c.1900, w. 5cm/2in, **£1,000–2,000/ $1,500–3,000**

▼ Silver, enamel & turquoise drop brooch

Charles Robert Ashbee (1863–1942) was one of the leading members of the Arts and Crafts movement. In 1888 he founded the Guild of Handicraft in London, but in 1902 it moved to Chipping Campden in the Cotswolds, Gloucestershire, where it survived until 1908. Ashbee's designs were often influenced by Art Nouveau. This brooch is unsigned but many were marked "G of H Ltd".

Silver, enamel and turquoise drop brooch by C.R. Ashbee and the Guild of Handicraft, 1900, 9cm/3.5in, **£2,000–5,000/$3,000–7,500**

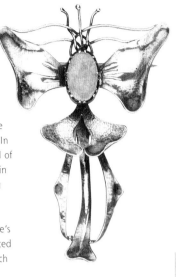

Silver and opal stylized insect brooch by C.R. Ashbee and the Guild of Handicraft, c.1900, l. 6cm/2½in, **£1,000–2,000/$1,500–3,000**

▲ Silver & opal stylized insect brooch

This Arts and Crafts brooch shows the influence of Art Nouveau in its dragonfly/butterfly motif. It also displays the typical Arts and Crafts feature of hand-hammered silver, interpreted in the USA by such designers as the Englishman William Christmas Codman, who produced an influential "Martelé" ("hammered") line for America's leading silversmiths, the Gorham Manufacturing Company.

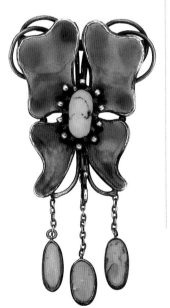

▼ Peacock pendant

The peacock motif, a favourite of C.R. Ashbee, was found in various sizes and materials, here in silver gilt, abalone (shell) and enamel. Perhaps the most spectacular example is the large peacock pendant brooch, in silver, gold, pearls and diamonds, made for his wife, Janet, on the occasion of their marriage, and now in the Victoria and Albert Museum, London.

Peacock pendant by C.R. Ashbee and the Guild of Handicraft, 1907, l. 6.5cm/2¾in, **£2,000–3,000/ $3,000–4,500**

Art Deco

Elegance, excitement, glamour: these are some of the qualities we associate today with the Art Deco movement, especially its jewellery. During the 1960s and 1970s, Art Deco jewellery became one of the most collectable jewellery categories of the 20thC, and remains so still. The style only acquired its name in the 1960s, however, in recognition of the importance of the *Exposition Internationale des Arts Decoratifs et Industriels Modernes* held in Paris in 1925, which was dedicated to works that showed "new inspiration and real originality". In subject-matter, style and colour, Art Deco furniture, jewellery, ceramics, posters and other decorative arts reflected the general atmosphere of optimism that prevailed after World War I. The liberation of women, the new jazz music, the preoccupation with travel and the rise of abstract art all influenced the designers of Art Deco.

▼ **Stylized face brooch**

Art Deco stylized face brooch, 1920s, l. 6cm/2¼in, **£150–200/ $225–300**

In the 1910s and 1920s, European avant-garde art was strongly influenced by African art, and African-inspired designs also eventually appeared as jewellery. The elongated and stylized design of this blue glass and marcasite brooch, unsigned but probably French, is taken from African masks. The brooch is of high quality, especially the glass components, which are specially designed rather than standard components fitted together. Of comparatively large size for a 1920s brooch, this might have been worn on an outer garment such as an opera coat.

▲ **French flower basket brooch**

A stylized interpretation of a traditional subject, here a flower basket, is typical of Art Deco design. This brooch is made in the "Cartier style", also called the "tutti-frutti" or "fruit salad" style. It imitates the pieces that Cartier made from the 1920s onwards, incorporating Indian tree-of-life designs and colours. The brooch is signed "France".

French Art Deco flower basket brooch, late 1920s, w. 5.5cm/2in, **£200–250/ $300–375**

French Art Deco silver and paste bracelet, 1920s/30s, l. 19cm/7½in, **£200–250/$300–375**

▲ Silver and paste bracelet

A fine example of French "all white" Art Deco jewellery at its most sophisticated, this was perhaps made as a "travelling" piece, in imitation of a diamond and platinum original left in the safe at home. Typical Art Deco features include its gently geometric shape, dense concentration of stones in contrasting baguette and brilliant cuts, and its overall emphasis on design rather than on individual stones. The bracelet is unsigned, but the sterling silver mount bears French hallmarks. Bracelets were the most popular Art Deco accessory, with several, often in different sizes, worn at the same time.

▼ Silver and paste necklace

The American company Coro, active between 1930 and 1960, was one of the most prolific designers of costume jewellery, and produced pieces in a broad variety of styles and price ranges. This necklace of sterling silver and green paste, originally part of a set, shows the classic ribbon motifs of Art Deco as well as a later "sunburst" motif. The piece is signed "Corocraft".

Art Deco silver and paste necklace by Coro, late 1930s, l. 42cm/16½in, **£150–200/$225–300**

American Art Deco

In 1924, the major Paris jewellery houses displayed their most up-to-date Art Deco creations at the Grand Central Palace in New York. These proved an inspiration to leading American jewellers such as Tiffany, Black, Starr & Frost, and Udall & Ballou, and were in turn copied by costume jewellers.

FACT FILE

Art Deco brooch by Fahrner, 1920s, 6.5cm/2½in, **£1,000–2,000/$1,500–3,000**

▲ Brooch by Fahrner

This small, intricate brooch is typical of the work of Theodor Fahrner – the most important German maker of costume jewellery. It combines marcasite with semi-precious stones (green chalcedony and blue amazonite) in a high-quality silver setting. Pieces by Fahrner signed with the initials "TF" in a circle are very collectable and fetch high prices in today's market.

Bakelite

Billed as "the material of a thousand uses", Bakelite was one of the most popular synthetic substances for making costume jewellery from the 1920s to the 1940s. It was discovered by Dr Leo Baekeland, a Belgian-born chemist living in New York, who was seeking a formula for synthetic shellac. Patented in 1907, it was widely used in industry for electrical insulation, radio and telephone casings and autoparts. From the 1920s its malleable "plastic" qualities and bright colours were prized by jewellery houses as illustrious as that of Lalique, who used it for a red, cherry-covered trinket box. Bakelite jewellery was also exhibited by the French designer Auguste Bonaz at the 1925 *Exposition Internationale des Arts Décoratifs*. Once its popularity spread, most pieces were left unsigned, so they can be difficult to identify without the help of a specialist dealer.

▶ **"Josephine Baker"**
In 1925 the dancer Josephine Baker took Paris by storm with her daring performances in the *Revue Nègre*, an African-American song-and-dance revue. Her jazz image appeared in paintings, decorative objects and jewellery of the period, especially in Bakelite or ceramic form. All of these pieces are highly collectable today. This brooch is French (signed "Déposé") and illustrates the European fashion for mixing Bakelite with other materials, here chrome. It is one of a number of articulated novelty brooches that appeared in the 1920s.

"Josephine Baker" Bakelite brooch, late 1920s, l. 8cm/3in, **£280–300/$420–450**

▼ **Art Deco brooch**
Bakelite adapts very well to the simple lines and geometric shapes of the Art Deco style. Here the striking colour contrasts are inspired by semi-precious substances such as jade, coral and amber. A vintage brooch such as this could easily be mistaken for a similar modern reproduction: specialist dealers can tell an original by patina, texture and even smell. Weight is also a guide, as modern pieces tend to be lighter.

Bakelite Art Deco brooch, 1920s, l. 7.5cm/3in, **£140–190/$210–285**

Bakelite bracelet with matching
clips, 1930s, bracelet
w. 9cm/3½in, clips w. 5cm/2in,
£400–450/$600–675

▲ **Bracelet & matching clips**
This chunky hinged bangle,
probably French, is an
example of the most sought-
after type of Bakelite
jewellery. The matching clips
give it added interest and
value. The green colour, in
imitation of jade, is one of
the most desirable shades,
as is the classic combination
of red and black. Bracelets
are perhaps the most popular
of all Bakelite pieces, and
are found carved in a wide
range of motifs (especially
floral and geometric).

▼ **Cherry brooch**
The craze for fruit and
vegetable jewellery was
inspired by costumes worn
by the Brazilian actress Carmen
Miranda. The flamboyant
designs were interpreted in
Bakelite as necklaces and
bracelets as well as brooches
in a variety of fruits, including
cherries, strawberries and
pineapples. In this piece the
cherries and leaves are hand-
carved and the stems are
made of plastic-coated string.
Always check these strings
are not cracked or peeling,
as this will lower the value.

Bakelite cherry brooch,
c.1940, l. 10cm/4in,
£200–250/$300–375

FACT FILE

Landmark sale
When Pop artist Andy
Warhol's collection
of Bakelite was sold in
1988, it became clear
how popular it had
become. Items such
as bangles, belt buckles,
clocks, radios and a
mini-collection of over
100 napkin rings sold
for more than ten times
their estimated value.

Bakelite "crib toy" necklace,
1940s, l. 5.5cm/2¼in,
£180–200/$270–300

▲ **"Crib toy" necklace**
An unusual design in Bakelite
and chrome, this is based on
a crib toy for a baby. The
ethnic theme often appears
in Bakelite pieces, and
other figures include black
American jazz musicians.
Figural Bakelite is highly
collectable, but beware of
fakes and modern versions.

1930s pot-metal enamels

In the 1930s the growth of mass-communication and the greater freedom and spending power of women produced an ever-expanding market for costume jewellery, especially if it captured the mood and style of precious jewellery. In both Europe and America an increasing number of designers used paste, plated metal and enamel to create a look that had immediate impact for less cash. The romantic films of Hollywood inspired a trend that harked back to a traditional, feminine style. By the late 1930s, the vogue for cameos and lockets was supplemented by a profusion of birds, baskets and floral sprays. Settings were often of a sculptural, curving femininity, and enamel flower brooches in pastel shades of powder blue, soft pink and pale green were particularly popular. These were traditionally inspired, often by Tiffany pieces of the late 19thC.

▼ **Lobster brooch**
The lobster was a favourite motif of the Surrealists, and was used by Salvador Dali in a design for an evening dress by Elsa Schiaparelli. It became a popular motif in Schiaparelli's costume jewellery, and was later freely adopted by other designers, along with more crustacea, such as sea-horses and crabs. This brooch is also found in a slightly more valuable version, with trembling claws.

Lobster brooch, 1930s, l. 8.5cm/3¼in, **£100–120/ $150–180**

▶ **Bird brooch**
Prized for its romantic associations with departure and the warm south, the swallow was a popular motif during the Victorian era. This 1930s version of a swallow brooch is unsigned and of fine quality. The use of milky pink cabochons is associated with Chanel's costume jewellery of the period, and this piece may be by her, or by a lesser French designer. The brooch has trembling wings, set on tiny springs that allow them to vibrate. "Trembling" jewels are a collector's category in their own right, as they are found in a variety of motifs from the 18thC onwards.

"Trembling" bird brooch, 1930s, w. 7.5cm/3in, **£160–180/ $240–270**

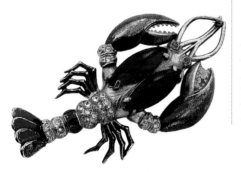

Checking condition

The condition of pot-metal enamels is very important: chipped or faded areas seriously lower value. Sometimes it is possible to retouch small areas with enamel model-making paints available in hobby and craft shops, if an exact colour match can be found. Restoration of larger areas is far less successful. A specialist dealer will advise.

▼ Basket of flowers brooch

The flower basket is one of the most popular jewellery motifs, reinterpreted in different designs and materials since the 18thC. It is a favourite collector's category, both signed and unsigned, and sometimes comes with matching earrings. This unsigned brooch would be attractive to a collector because of its good condition, skilful combination of materials and cuts of paste, and its graceful design with curving scrolls that anticipate the designs of the 1940s.

Basket of flowers brooch,
1930s, w. 7.5cm/3in
£150–200/$225–300

▼ Chanel iris brooch

In 1935 one of Chanel's most famous designers, Fulco di Verdura (later to become a leading jeweller) created a red enamel rose brooch for her. This signalled the beginning of a soft, romantic mood, culminating in her "Bijoux de Fleurs" ("Flower Jewellery") series, made by Maison Gripoix in the late 1930s. Although the flowers were scrupulously based on natural forms, Chanel liked to experiment with non-naturalistic colour – here with a pale purple iris. It is signed "Chanel" in script signature.

Chanel iris brooch,
1930s, l. 7.5cm/3in
£400–500/$600–750

▼ Butterfly brooch

This is another 1930s unsigned brooch whose design antici-pates the 1940s trend of focusing on a single high-quality stone: here, a large square-cut imitation amethyst. Butterfly brooches form part of the category of insect jewellery, popular from the mid 19thC onwards, and inspired by an increasing interest in natural history. Check the condition carefully – delicate legs and antennae are especially vulnerable.

Butterfly brooch, 1930s,
w. 7.5cm/3in
**£150–200/
$225–300**

Double clips

It is said that the idea of clip brooches came to the French jeweller Louis Cartier as he idly watched a peasant woman hanging out her washing with wooden clothes pegs. He then developed a series of clips and double clips, patenting the double clip in 1927. This versatile piece came with a frame fitted with an ordinary brooch pin, so that the clips could also be worn together as a single brooch. It quickly gained popularity, and was made in a wide range of styles in both Europe and the USA. According to the leader of fashion Loelia, Duchess of Westminster: "By the end of the Twenties it had become essential to possess a pair of diamond, or pseudo-diamond, clips. They were clipped not only to hats but on to everything else, even the small of the back, where they served to keep underclothes out of sight." Double clips remained popular until the 1950s, graduating in style from geometric, Art Deco forms towards a chunkier, more sculptural naturalism.

CoroDuette double clip, 1940s, w. 5cm/2in (the pair), **£650–700/ $975–1,050**

▶ **Frog Duette**
Coro was the first major American costume jewellery manufacturer to make double clips, and its line of "Duettes" did much to spread the fame of the firm. Coro was particularly well known for its animal and floral clips, popular with today's collectors. The frog motif, interpreted by both Coro and Trifari, is one of the most collectable novelties of the 1940s. The ingeniously designed detachable brooch frame is pictured here with the clips.

▼ **"Tutti-frutti" double clip**
Double clips were not solely made by Coro – Trifari, Mazer and Boucher were also leading manufacturers. Trifari produced some figural pieces but concentrated more on purely abstract double-clip designs. This mid-1930s double clip was designed by Alfred Philippe in imitation of Cartier's "tutti-frutti" style. It is signed "KTF", an early Trifari mark reserved for pieces of the very highest quality. It came with matching necklace and bracelet, and is now a very collectable piece.

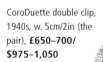

Trifari "tutti frutti" double clip, 1930s, w. 7cm/2¾in, **£350–400/ $525–600**

CoroDuette "Camellia" double
clip, 1930s, w. 8cm/3in,
£350–400/$525–600

▲ "Camellia" Duette

An outstanding early example
of a double clip, incorporating
many of the features of
precious jewellery. The mixture
of different cuts of stone
(baguette and brilliant) is
typical of the 1930s. For
the imitation rubies, Coro has
used the technique of "invisible
setting" introduced by the
French fine jewellers Van Cleef
& Arpels in the 1930s, in
which small squares of stones
are fastened from the back
and look as if there
were no metal
mount. The
flowers have
"trembler"
heads.

▼ Large paste double clip

A typical Art Deco design,
here in paste. Unsigned, the
small size and delicacy of
the stones suggests French
manufacture. Although it
has a classic, decorative
design, it would be of little
interest to a collector: it is
missing its backing, so it
functions as two single clips
only. It also has several "dead"
stones, where the backing has
separated from the stone and
the stone has darkened.

Large paste double clip,
1930s, w. 9.5cm/3¾in,
£100–150/$150–225

Imitation aquamarine and paste
double clip, 1930s, w. 8cm/3in,
£160–180/$240–270

▲ "Aquamarine" double clip

This is an attractive, unsigned
double clip, probably French.
Aquamarines were one of the
most popular gemstones of
the 1930s, used extensively
by Cartier, and especially
appreciated by their American
clients. In 1935 Elsie de
Wolfe, the trendsetting
American socialite, ordered
a diamond and aquamarine
tiara from Cartier, and had
her hair tinted to match.

Trifari

In 1904, Gustavo Trifari, who was descended from a long line of jewellers, left Naples for New York, where he worked with his uncle making costume jewellery. In 1912 he began operating under his own name, producing hair ornaments and accessories. The salesman Leo Krussman joined Trifari in 1917, and the reputation of Trifari jewels started to grow. The firm was officially founded in 1925 by Gustavo Trifari, Leo Krussman and Carl M. Fishel. In 1930 they hired the French designer Alfred Philippe, whose elegant and innovative ideas were to contribute greatly to the success of the company. From 1930 onwards, the firm created a huge array of costume jewellery at a level that has yet to be surpassed. Trifari jewels were made for Broadway musicals in the 1930s, and their popularity caused department stores nationwide to carry their lines. Today Trifari remains one of the largest American manufacturers of costume jewellery.

▼ **"Floraleaf" brooch**

"Floraleaf" was one of Trifari's leading ranges of 1948, featuring typical high-quality moulded paste in the tradition of the "tutti frutti" style (see p.27). In this piece clusters of milky-coloured paste flowers imitate moonstones. A version of this brooch was also made with pale blue flowers, imitating chalcedony. The metal used is the alloy trifanium, specially created for Trifari to create a non-tarnishing but real gold effect.

"Floraleaf" brooch, 1948, w. 5cm/2in, **£160–200/ $240–300**

▼ **"Jelly Belly" frog brooch**

Unlike many other costume jewellers, Trifari maintained production during World War II, and produced some spectacular vermeil brooches (see pp.34–5), both abstract and figural – the best known being the "Jelly Belly" series. These were developed from an animal series of the 1930s, which used large high-quality paste central stones for the "bellies". Owing to the wartime scarcity of pastes, Alfred Philippe used the more readily available solid clear plastic lucite, which closely resembled rock-crystal.

"Jelly Belly" frog brooch, 1940s, l. 6.5cm/2½in, **£650–700/ $975–1,050**

Collecting "Jelly Bellies"

"Jelly Bellies" are a popular collecting field, and subjects include birds, seals, elephants, pekinese dogs, and insects such as bees, which tend to be less valuable than the "cuter" animals (owls are considered unlucky). Jelly Bellies were made for several decades, but only the vermeil silver pieces command top prices.

▼ Pink glass brooch & earrings set

At the beginning of the 1940s Alfred Philippe created a unique collection of delicate floral designs in pastel shades such as pink, lilac and ivory. This brooch and earrings set, which probably also had a matching necklace, is a more mass-produced version of the *pâte-de-verre* or "glass paste" flower pieces that Maison Gripoix created for Chanel from the late 1930s. Alfred Philippe had designed precious jewellery for both Cartier and Van Cleef & Arpels and was much influenced by French design. In the 1950s he created a similar "Wild Flowers" collection, using enamel flowers.

Pink glass brooch and earrings, 1940s, brooch w. 8.5cm/ 3¼in, earrings w. 3.5cm/1⅜in, **£200–250/$300–375**

Crown brooch, 1941, w. 5cm/2in, **£250–300/$375–450**

▲ Crown brooch

From 1936–7, when the "KTF" mark was discontinued, the crown became part of Trifari's trademark and the crown brooch was one of their most famous successes. Devised in 1941, the brooch was produced in both silver and base metal, the silver being the more valuable. Unlike the Edwardian version (see p.14), which refers to the design of a real crown, Trifari crown brooches were created in a range of fantasy designs and colours such as red, green and deep blue. The "Coronation Gems" of 1953 (see p.30) followed slightly more historic designs.

▼ Pink pressed glass necklace

This is another piece that uses glass paste inspired by Indian "tutti frutti" designs, here in an exotic shade of pink that is popular with collectors. Carved or pressed glass jewellery by Trifari is scarce and valuable. Care must be taken, however, as losing one of the glass pieces will lower the value significantly. These glass pieces are difficult to match, but repair is possible if you are lucky enough to find a similar item.

Pink pressed glass necklace, early 1950s, l. 42cm/16½in, **£180–200/$270–300**

▼ Orb brooch

Part of the "Coronation Gems" series of 1953 commemorating the coronation of Queen Elizabeth II, this brooch made of trifanium and brightly coloured pastes was a development on the earlier crown brooches (see p.29). The series included an orb, crown and sceptre set, all with earrings in complementary shapes. Similar jewels were made by Coro. From the early 1950s Trifari jewels were sold in the UK, at first in the showrooms of Norman Hartnell, the Queen's dressmaker, and later in leading department stores.

Trifari orb brooch, 1953, l. 5cm/2in, **£150–200/$225–300**

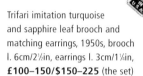

Trifari imitation turquoise and sapphire leaf brooch and matching earrings, 1950s, brooch l. 6cm/2⅜in, earrings l. 3cm/1¼in, **£100–150/$150–225** (the set)

▲ Imitation turquoise & sapphire leaf brooch and earrings set

The leaf brooch was a perennially popular Trifari shape, made in different designs and materials from the late 1940s. This matching set is made with cabochon, rather than faceted pastes, which is rare, and suggests an Indian influence. It still bears its original paper tag, which adds to the value. Trifari collectors seek high-quality, typical pieces in good condition, such as these. A full parure can be found in internet auctions on specialist jewellery sites.

▼ Leaf garland bracelet & earrings

From the early 1960s, Trifari expanded its range of costume jewellery to reflect the diversity of 1960s styles, while also developing traditional, sophisticated ranges in "brushed gold", high-quality coloured pastes and diamanté. This bracelet and matching earrings are part of a full parure comprising a matching necklace and brooch. Its good condition and colour combination of deep blue and green make it a desirable collector's item. As always, pieces with coloured pastes tend to be more valuable than pieces that are all diamanté.

Trifari leaf garland bracelet and matching earrings, early 1960s, bracelet l. 17.5cm/7in, earrings w. 2.5cm/1in, **£160–200/$240–300**

A legal matter
There was fierce competition between Trifari and Coro, its largest rival; they made near identical pieces such as hand, crown and "Jelly-Belly" brooches. In 1955, in a landmark case, Trifari obtained a court judgement against Coro. It established fashion jewellery design as a work of art, and thus worthy of copyright.

▼ "Brushed gold" & imitation pearl bracelet

Trifari was always famed for its high-quality imitation pearls, given a public seal of approval in 1953 and 1957 when America's First Lady, Mamie Eisenhower, commissioned Alfred Philippe to create a "pearl" parure for the presidential inaugural balls. (The Smithsonian Institute, Washington, D.C. has copies of the jewels.) This "brushed gold" and imitation pearl bracelet, part of a complete parure, is one of a very popular type produced and sold in large quantities from the early 1950s through to the 1970s, and therefore not unusual and still modestly priced. Trifari jewels tend to lose individual pearls, but unlike Haskell pearls these are of a standard type and easy to replace.

Trifari "brushed gold" and imitation pearl bracelet, 1960s, l. 18cm/7in, **£30–40/$45–60**

Trifari sea-horse brooch by André Boeuf, 1968, diam. 8cm/3in, **£300–350/$450–525**

▲ Sea-horse brooch

In line with its expansion in the 1960s, Trifari increased its talented design team. In 1967 André Boeuf joined Trifari, having trained at Cartier in Paris, and he remained with the company until 1979, replacing Alfred Philippe as head designer when he retired in 1968. This sea-horse brooch shows the influence of the fantasy jewels created by the New York jeweller Jean Schlumberger, who had worked with Schiaparelli and later became head of design at Tiffany's, New York.

Trifari multicoloured floral brooch and earrings, early 1960s, brooch w. 6cm/2⅜in, earrings w. 3.5cm/1¼in, **£180–200/$270–300**

▲ Multicoloured floral brooch and earrings set

Another innovative style of the 1960s, this is highly collectable as it has many coloured paste stones. Such a set probably came with a matching necklace and bracelet; having a full set would enhance the value of each individual piece. Check that all the stones are present, as they can be very difficult to replace. This busy pastel colour scheme is quite rare, as Trifari usually favoured more straightforward colours.

Hollywood jewels

The stars of Hollywood's Golden Age, the 1930s and 1940s, created a mini jewellery industry of their own. "For a whole seven days, I promise you a wonderful piece of jewellery before breakfast, before lunch and before dinner", wrote Howard Hughes to Ava Gardner (she refused his offer). Although Marlene Dietrich wore her personal jewellery – most memorably, a spectacular French Art Deco bracelet – in the Hitchcock film *Stage Fright*, jewellery for major films was usually specially commissioned from leading manufacturers in Hollywood and New York. It was made in paste, and often recreated in commercial ranges sold through smart boutiques and department stores. The designer Eugene Joseff rented, rather than sold, his pieces, amassing a collection of some three million pieces that are now of great value as a research archive.

◀ **Corocraft hand brooch**
Coro was the largest American manufacturer of costume jewellery. This brooch, one of the firm's most recognizable pieces, is part of a "Friendship Set", which includes a matching ring, and is by Adolf Katz, one of Coro's leading designers. It was used in a publicity campaign for Coro in 1945. Made of vermeil silver (see pp.34–5), it has a chunky three-dimensional quality that is considered highly desirable. The bracelet trim, with its square-cut imitation aquamarine, is typical of the retro style of the 1940s.

Corocraft hand brooch, 1944, l. 6.5cm/2½in, **£400–450/ $600–675**

▼ **Hobé basket brooch**
William Hobé, descended from a family of French fine jewellers, was one of the leading designers commissioned to create costume jewels for the "historic" films popular in Hollywood. His company specialized in these silver flower-spray pieces, blossoming with tiny closed silver buds and flowers of paste or semi-precious stones, all hand-made using traditional techniques of metalworking and gem-setting, and given a sought-after "antique" effect. Hobé basket brooches are very collectable, as are handbag frames with similar fine metalwork.

Hobé basket brooch, 1940s, l. 7.5cm/3in, **£150–200/ $225–300**

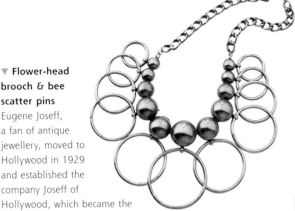

▼ Flower-head brooch & bee scatter pins

Eugene Joseff, a fan of antique jewellery, moved to Hollywood in 1929 and established the company Joseff of Hollywood, which became the leading supplier of costume jewellery to the film industry. This brooch and scatter pins are typical of his pieces of the 1940s. They came with earrings to match, and are made with a typical coppery gold matte finish, known as "Russian" gold plating, which minimized the glare from the powerful studio lights. Joseff's pieces appear in such classic films as *Gone with the Wind* (1939) and *Cleopatra* (1962).

Joseff brooch & scatter pins, 1940s, brooch diam. 7.5cm/3in, pins w. 3.5cm/1⅜in, **£300–500/ $450–750**

Joseff of Hollywood hoop necklace, 1940s, l. 45cm/17¾in, **£550–600/$825–900**

▲ Hoop necklace

The film star Anne Sheridan was photographed wearing this striking gold-plated necklace in "gypsy" mood. This piece is typical of Joseff's ability to simplify particular historical styles and give them a "larger-than-life" quality that instantly conveyed the appropriate historical feel on the big screen. Joseff was one of the few jewellers to make plain metal pieces (i.e. no pastes), and pieces that had no more than one or two large and simple stones. Joseff jewellery can be spoiled by over-cleaning: a wipe with a tissue will maintain the desired patina.

▼ Coro blowfish pin

Coro produced a huge variety of jewellery styles that differed enormously in quality and were aimed at a wide range of customers. This silver enamelled fantasy fish is among the most collectable Coro pieces, along with retro bracelets and double clips (see pp.26–7). The company used approximately 50 different trademarks between 1930 and 1960, but Coro, CoroCraft and CoroDuette are the most important.

Coro blowfish pin, 1940s, 8.5cm/3¼in, **£300–350/$450–525**

Vermeil

The outbreak of World War II had a profound effect on the US fashion and jewellery industries, cutting off clothing and jewellery imports, and inspiring designers to create truly American styles. When the USA entered the war in December 1941, the government imposed many restrictions on raw materials to concentrate on the war effort, and ironically this resulted in some of the most fabulous and collectable costume jewellery of the century. The most important restriction was the substitution of sterling silver for the various base metals previously used. From 1942 most American costume jewellery made of metal was "vermeil" silver, i.e. silver plated with gold. This gold plating, named from the French for "rosy", was much thicker and more long-lasting than on later costume jewellery, and gave a characteristic rich, warm finish. Most genuine American vermeil pieces are stamped "sterling" meaning sterling silver; they may also bear a manufacturer's mark.

Vermeil mandarin brooch by Reja, 1940s, l. 6.5cm/2⅛in, **£600–700/ $900–1,050**

▼ Mandarin brooch

The vermeil brooch or clip was the most popular lapel decoration for the tailored, almost mannish fashions of the time, and best epitomizes the wartime period. The New York-based costume jewellery company, Reja, produced a wide range of superb figural vermeil brooches, now highly collectable. Some of Reja's most distinctive pieces, such as this one, are inspired by masks, and include a range of exotic and novelty subjects such as African, Indian and clown motifs.

▶ Vermeil fish brooch

The uniformity of wartime dressing led to a craving for novelty and whim, so the range of brooch ideas was widened to include an enormous variety of figural motifs. Animals, birds, insects and fish were all popular, usually in a stylized, rounded shape, and sparingly set with coloured paste gems. Paste and diamanté from Europe were severely rationed, and manufacturers had to rely on their own back stocks, or use coloured glass stones made in the USA.

Vermeil fish brooch by Reja, 1940s, w. 4cm/1½in, **£150–200/ $225–300**

▲ Fly brooch

This is one of a range of vermeil figural brooches launched by Reja in spring/summer 1945 (the other subjects were a lizard, a flamingo, a pheasant and a butterfly). Each creature was set with large central coloured pastes. Reja was founded in the early 1930s by Solomon Finkelstein, its director until its closure in 1954. It was first named the Solomon Finkelstein Co., becoming Deja Costume Jewelry Inc. in 1939. This led to an injunction from Du Jay Inc., a larger manufacturer of costume jewellery, so it was finally re-named Reja.

Vermeil fly brooch by Reja, 1945, w. 3.5cm/1¼in, **£70–100/$105–150**

▼ Floral brooch

The firm Frank A. J. Pennino was founded in New York in 1926. In 1932 the company became Pennino Bros. During World War II, under the management of Oreste Pennino, it concentrated on producing a range of vermeil brooches, now considered very collectable. They are usually of delicate flower, bow and abstract motifs, often trailing ribbon-like tendrils of curving metal, and also in typical 1940s designs of drapery-like folds, scrolls, pleats and ruffles.

Vermeil floral brooch by Pennino, 1940s, w. 8.5cm/3⅜in, **£460–500/$690–750**

FACT FILE

Cocktail Style

The Cocktail Style of the 1940s, named after the cocktail parties that became a popular social event, inspired a style of jewellery often interpreted in vermeil. Characteristics include:
- a bold sculptural quality
- use of large gold or vermeil surfaces
- single paste stones in strong colours, sometimes trimmed with diamanté.

Vermeil retro-style bracelet by Mazer, 1940s, l. 17.5cm/6¾in, **£200–250/$300–375**

▲ Retro-style bracelet

Chunky, one-off bracelets were also widely made in vermeil. In the late 1930s and 1940s retro, or retro moderne, developed from Art Deco machine-age forms. Pieces were large and dramatic, incorporating geometric shapes of circles, squares and cylinders. The emphasis was on a large square-cut stone, or a succession of stones. Founded in the 1920s, the firm of Mazer (later Jomaz) created some stunning "Cocktail Style" pieces.

Designer jewellery

The dovetailing of fashion and jewellery that we know today was born in the 1920s. When Mrs Wallis Simpson wore some spectacular sapphire and diamond jewels given to her by the Prince of Wales, an observer recorded erroneously that they were "dressmaker's jewels". Fashion designers employed highly skilled jewellery manufacturers, such as Maison Gripoix of Paris, to produce costume jewellery that was aimed at those who already owned genuine jewels. It could echo designs in precious jewellery, or be more experimental, and it created a whole "look", with every detail perfect. Sometimes, the piece was supplied with the dress, and sometimes later developed into a range manufactured under licence. Two legendary Paris-based designers led this trend: Coco Chanel (1883–1971) and Elsa Schiaparelli (1890–1973).

◀ **Schiaparelli earrings**
In the 1930s Elsa Schiaparelli's costume jewellery was zany and playful, revealing the influence of her friends in the Surrealist movement, and was made in extremely limited quantities. Today's collector is more likely to concentrate on her later pieces, produced under licence after her move to the USA in the 1950s. These show her love of experimentation, her use of abstract shapes and organic forms such as shells and snails, and of "fantasy" pastes, i.e. iridescent, oddly coloured gemstones, not based on real ones. These earrings are signed "Schiaparelli" in script.

Schiaparelli shell earrings, late 1950s, d. 4cm/1½in, **£200–250/ $300–375**

▼ **Hattie Carnegie pin**
The Vienna-born American fashion designer Hattie Carnegie designed costume jewellery from the 1930s to the 1950s to complement her "Little Carnegie Suit" and other fashion creations. There is no typical look to her designs but she produced a feminine, elegant range of flower and figural brooches. Her pieces are signed "HC", "Carnegie", or "Hattie Carnegie".

Hattie Carnegie hand-beaded pin, 1940s, l. 5.5cm/2¼in, **£80–90/ $120–135**

Couturiers
In the 1950s couturiers opened "ready to wear" boutiques that also sold costume jewellery. Collectable names are:
Cristobal Balenciaga (1895–1972)
Christian Dior (*see* p.44)
Jacques Fath (1912–54)
Hubert de Givenchy (b.1927)
Norman Hartnell (1901–79)

▼ Chanel star brooch

The timeless elegance of Coco Chanel is seen in a whole range of costume jewellery that she designed from the 1920s to complement the plain lines and colours of her clothes. In the early 1930s she was particularly inspired by the star motif, creating with the designer Paul Iribe a line of precious jewels with stars, crescents and comets of diamonds. This exquisite "shooting star" brooch is made in characteristic honey-coloured gold metal. As with most *bijoux de couture*, it is unsigned.

Chanel shooting star brooch, 1930s, l. 11.5cm/4½in,
£2,500–3,000/$3,750–4,500

Schiaparelli leaf bracelet, 1950s, l. 20cm/8in,
£300–400/$450–600

▲ Schiaparelli leaf bracelet

The use of frosted glass leaves is a typical feature of Schiaparelli's pieces of the 1950s made in the USA. This bracelet is part of a complete parure of necklace, earrings, bracelet and brooch, also made in clear, brown and red versions. As always with unusual pastes, once cracked or broken these glass leaves are irreplaceable and will seriously affect the value. It is signed "Schiaparelli" in script. Fakes are common, so check the signature carefully: sometimes the name is misspelt, or more blurred and harder to read than the original.

▼ Chanel brooch

One of Chanel's perennial inspirations in her costume jewellery was the magnificence of Renaissance jewellery, with its dangling components and richly coloured cabochon stones. Here the style is imitated in high-quality *pâte-de-verre*. The honey-coloured "old gold" setting and filigree backings are also typical of early Chanel designs.

Chanel brooch, 1960s, l. 7.5cm/3in,
£800–1,000/$1,200–1,500

Eisenberg

The Eisenberg firm was founded in Chicago in 1914 by Jonas Eisenberg as a quality clothing company for women. Jonas's two sons, Harold and Sam, continued the clothing line in the 1930s, changing the label from Eisenberg & Sons to Eisenberg Originals. Many of the items were accessorized with clips, brooches and buckles of the firm's own design: bold, dramatic and finely crafted pieces that became so popular in their own right that they were often pilfered from the dresses on the saleroom floors. This led the Eisenberg brothers in 1935 to commission a New York manufacturer to produce costume jewellery accessories, which would co-ordinate with their dresses but would be sold separately and only by very exclusive shops. By 1958 the Eisenbergs abandoned their clothing line to concentrate solely on costume jewellery, which the company continues to produce successfully today.

▼ Fur clip

This bold sophisticated fur clip, made of base metal and high-quality Swarovski imitation diamonds and sapphires (glass crystal stones manufactured by Daniel Swarovski in the Tyrol), is typical of some of Eisenberg's most collectable pieces. The fur clip has a strong double prong for fixing the brooch to a fur coat or thick outer garment. Prices for Eisenberg brooches of this period have risen considerably since the 1980s, both in Europe and the USA, which has led to many imitations being made. The best guide is weight: a genuine Eisenberg will be dense and heavy for its size.

"Eisenberg Original" fur clip, early 1940s, l. 8cm/3in, **£200–250/$300–375**

Leaf brooch, 1940s, l. 9.5cm/ 3¾in, **£250–275/$375–415**

◄ Leaf brooch

When the USA entered World War II in 1941 base metals were needed for the manufacture of armaments, so Eisenberg concentrated on a range of jewels made in sterling silver, which are particularly prized today. In spite of its large size, this silver brooch has a light, delicate quality that would have beautifully set off an Eisenberg gown. The design anticipates the sharper, floral shapes of the 1950s, and there were also versions made with high-quality imitation emerald and topaz stones.

Identifying Eisenberg
Precise dating of
Eisenberg pieces can
be difficult, as marks
overlapped, but the
most usual are:
• "Eisenberg Original" –
from the 1930s and
early 1940s.
• the single letter "E" –
probably the mid-1940s.
• "Eisenberg Ice" –
the late 1940s up
until the present day.

"Eisenberg Original"
fur clip, 1940s, l. 6.5cm/2½in,
£300–350/$450–525

▲ **1940s fur clip**
Another piece made in silver,
this clip has a radiating
starburst design. Such a
design, with a large central
stone as a focal point, is
typical of the 1940s. Again,
the stones are particularly
high-quality Swarovski
imitation rubies and diamanté,
the rubies of a navette (boat-
shaped) cut. Similar pieces
were also made with clear
diamanté and imitation
emeralds and sapphires (the
all-white diamanté pieces are
considered the least valuable
today). Clips and brooches
are the most common
"Eisenberg Original" pieces,
although necklaces, bracelets
and rings are also found.

"Eisenberg Ice" Christmas tree
brooch, 1970s, l. 5.5cm/2¼in,
£70–100/$105–150

▲ **Christmas tree brooch**
Christmas tree brooches
appeared in the USA from the
early 1950s, made especially
to send to servicemen in
the Korean War. Since then
they have been produced by
leading jewellery-makers in
a vast range of sizes, styles
and designs as an annual
novelty, and have become
increasingly popular items to
collect. One private collector
in Minnesota owns over
3,000 examples.

▼ **"Eisenberg Ice" earrings**
Eisenberg's later pieces used
smaller, brighter pastes, still
from Swarovski, and light-weight
rhodium (silvery-white metal)
settings to epitomize the "glitz"
style of the 1950s, also typified
by designers such as Weiss (see
pp.46–7). This popular design
was made in a full range of
pieces (necklaces, bracelets
and brooches), and in a
variety of colours, including
pink, green, red and blue,
as well as in a clear version.
A good starting point for
a new collector would be
to piece together a matching
set: a complete one would
be worth over £300 ($450).

Pair of "Eisenberg Ice" earrings,
late 1950s, l. 3cm/1¼in,
£60–70/$90–105

Miriam Haskell

Miriam Haskell made some of the most beautiful, collectable and valuable of all American costume jewellery. She was born in Indiana, in 1899, and studied at the University of Chicago from 1918-21, majoring in education. By 1924 she had moved to New York, and opened a small shop in the smart McAlpine Hotel, selling original, handmade jewellery inspired by natural motifs such as flowers, shells and leaves. By 1926 her work was in demand from retailers, and she established the Miriam Haskell company. The 1930s saw increasing expansion, and by the late 1940s and 1950s the company was producing the range of jewels that are so sought after now. Haskell became ill in 1952 and control of the firm changed several times. In 1989 it was bought by a firm based in Rhode Island that today still produces jewels under the Miriam Haskell name.

▲ Brooch and earrings set
This brooch and earrings made of "antique Russian gold", diamanté and tiny imitation seed pearls have the distinctive look considered to be classic Haskell by today's collectors. Pastes and imitation pearls were handwired onto a filigree backing using a technique more like needlework than gem-setting. The rich "gold" finish is a Haskell formula: a fusion of gold and silver on a brass and copper base.

Matching brooch and earrings, mid-1940s/1950s, brooch w. 7cm/ 2¾in, earrings w. 3.5cm/1¼in, **£850–1,000/ $1,275– 1,500**

▼ Pair of pendant earrings
As with the brooch and earrings set, left, this pair of earrings displays the most desirable combination of imitation pearl, paste and old gold. Long pendant earrings by Haskell are amongst the most sought-after pieces, and they come in a wide variety of styles. Check the pearls for any peeling and the metal for greening (verdigris), both of which will negatively affect the value of the piece.

Pair of pendant earrings, 1950s, l. 6cm/2¼in, **£175–200/ $265–300**

▼ Stickpin

In 1960 Robert F. Clark took over from Frank Hess as chief designer, and in 1961 became Vice-President of the Haskell firm until 1967. During the 1960s the company continued to make its classic collectable styles, but also developed ranges in a more contemporary idiom. This 1960s stickpin, a good choice for a novice collector, still features the typical filigree backing, matt gold finish and high-quality paste, and bears the Miriam Haskell stamp on the back of the flower head. Up to the late 1940s some pieces were unsigned; those items that are may have a horseshoe-shaped signature plaque, or the wartime dove of peace.

Stickpin, 1960s, l. 7.5cm/3in, **£40–60/$60–90**

From the late 1940s, most Haskell jewellery bears this oval stamp. The metal on new pieces has a shinier yellow finish than the soft antique-looking matt gold of earlier items.

Silver metal and imitation pearl necklace by "Robert", early 1950s, l. 39cm/15½in, **£250–300/$375–450**

▲ Silver metal & imitation pearl necklace by "Robert"

Haskell's great success inspired a "school of Haskell" group of designers, including Robert de Mario, who had worked with her. His pieces have also become collectable and are signed "Robert", "Demario", or "Original by Robert". This necklace is part of a full parure of necklace, earrings, brooch and bracelet in which not all pieces are signed, as opposed to Haskell parures of the 1950s, where every piece is signed. As with Haskell's jewellery, silver metal is considered slightly less desirable than a gold finish.

Haskell in World War II

With the restriction on the use of base metals during the war, Haskell used a variety of natural, readily available materials to make jewellery that is now highly sought after by collectors. These materials include: wood, plastic, Bakelite, leather and even scales of pine cones and dried broad beans.

Leaf bangle bracelet, c.1950, diam. 7.5cm/3in, **£150–175/$225–265**

▲ Leaf bangle bracelet

This plain "gold" Haskell bracelet is rare and desirable. The leaf design was repeated in various pieces, including choker necklaces, sautoirs (long necklaces) and earrings. Haskell made a series of decorated rigid bangle bracelets, all signed inside with the distinctive Haskell plate and all with a safety chain.

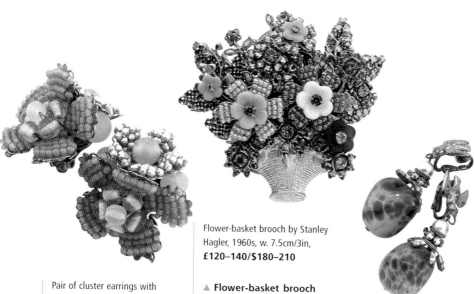

Flower-basket brooch by Stanley Hagler, 1960s, w. 7.5cm/3in, **£120–140/$180–210**

Pair of cluster earrings with pastel-coloured flowers, 1950s, w. 4cm/1½in, **£120–130/$180–195**

Pair of Murano glass earrings, 1950s, l. 5cm/2in, **£90–120/$135–180**

▲ Pair of cluster earrings
Although the traditional Haskell combination of old gold, imitation pearl and diamanté is most sought after, Haskell's reputation also rests on the huge range of colours in her jewels. Soft pastel shades commonly appeared in her spring/summer collections, using high-quality *pâte-de-verre* beads, probably French. As the 1950s progressed, colours became bolder and sharper; the May 1961 cover of American *Vogue* shows the film star Sophia Loren wearing a pair of all-black Haskell cluster earrings.

▲ Flower-basket brooch
The New York costume jeweller Stanley Hagler now has an international reputation. His fascination with jewellery started when he worked briefly as a business adviser for Miriam Haskell, after which he was inspired to create his own pieces. Like Haskell, he favours handwired components on a filigree backing, but his pieces are bigger and more opulent, with brighter colours. He made these flower baskets from the 1960s to the 1980s, always signing them "Stanley Hagler NYC".

▲ Pair of Murano glass earrings
From the late 1930s, Miriam Haskell and her chief designer Frank Hess made regular trips to Europe to select the finest components for Haskell jewellery. The glass factories of Murano, near Venice, whose glass-making tradition dates back to the 14thC, were a regular destination. Haskell pioneered the use of Murano glass beads in high-fashion jewellery, and recently pieces incorporating Murano beads in bright colours such as pink, red, citrine and cobalt blue have become popular with collectors.

Silver metal and white moulded glass flower brooch, early 1960s, w. 6.5cm/2½in, **£30–50/$45–75**

Haskell & Joan Crawford

The film star Joan Crawford was one of Miriam Haskell's most loyal celebrity customers from the 1930s to the late 1960s. Following the actress's death in 1977, her extensive collection of Haskell pieces, together with other jewellery, was sold at auction by the Plaza Art Gallery, New York, in January 1978.

FACT FILE

▼ Double-strand imitation pearl necklace

Haskell is especially famed for her superb imitation pearls, imported from Japan from the late 1940s on. They differ from European examples in the lustre of their surface, achieved through up to 12 immersions in *essence d'orient* – a substance made of fish scales, cellulose and acrylic resins. Colours range from white, champagne and pink, to shades of grey and a rich chocolate. Clasps are varied in shape and beautifully worked: the more elaborate, the higher the price.

Double-strand imitation pearl necklace, 1950s, l. 64cm/25¼in, **£220–280/$330–420**

▲ Silver metal & white moulded glass flower brooch

Fashions come and go in colours, often for no apparent reason. Currently plain white, as opposed to clear diamanté, is the least collectable of all colours. This is true for all 20thC costume jewellery, the only exception being the black-and-white Op Art colour schemes of the 1960s. This pretty white brooch, in good condition, is priced much lower than a comparable coloured piece, and could represent a good opportunity for a novice collector.

Green textured glass drop necklace, 1950s, l. 42cm/16½in, **£190–230/$285–345**

▶ Green textured glass drop necklace

This dramatic piece, focusing on a single high-quality glass stone, is carved in imitation Chinese jade. Haskell necklaces can be signed in up to three places: on an oval plate on the reverse of a pendant, as it is here; on the clasp, again as it is here; and with an additional oval signature plate dangling from the chain and attached by a jump ring. Never accept a piece as properly signed if it only has the third type of signature, as the plate can easily be a substitution from a genuine Haskell piece.

Christian Dior

In February 1947, Christian Dior, an almost unknown Frenchman aged 40, opened his own fashion house in the Avenue Montaigne, Paris, revealing for the first time the flowing, feminine lines of what came to be known as the "New Look". Although Dior's extravagant use of fabric was controversial (a photography session was mobbed by women screaming "40,000 francs for a dress, and our children have no milk!"), it had a huge impact and was copied worldwide as a much-needed antidote to wartime austerity. Dior's costume jewellery, created freshly for each twice-yearly collection, played an important part. While some pieces accentuated the romantic, feminine mood, others were an adventurous foil to more formal, tailored clothes. It was manufactured by several outside companies, but most pieces were designed by Dior himself, who maintained strict quality control.

Blue paste and imitation pearl brooch, 1959, w. 6.5cm/2½in, **£180–220/$270–330**

▶ **Blue paste and imitation pearl brooch**
This brooch is typical of much of Dior's costume jewellery, with its clusters of iridescent petal-shaped pastes, and high-quality rhodium plating. It probably came with a matching necklace or earrings (bracelets are rare). It was made by the German firm of Henkel & Grosse, which in 1955 was granted a licence to be exclusive producers of Dior's designs. Their pieces are marked (Christian Dior or Chr. Dior) and dated, unusually for costume jewellery, which makes them particularly satisfying to the historically minded collector.

▼ **Coloured paste & imitation pearl fish brooch**
This is a rare figural subject for a brooch by Henkel & Grosse. Other Dior figural brooches include a "Circus" series, also by Henkel & Grosse, and a unicorn series by Mitchel Maer, an English designer who made costume jewellery for Dior in the early 1950s. Christian Dior died in 1957, but the young Yves Saint Laurent and other designers continued to produce Dior's jewellery, reworking and developing Dior's main themes.

Coloured paste and imitation pearl fish brooch, 1961, w. 7cm/2¾in, **£350–400/$525–600**

▼ Turquoise & citrine paste brooch

The New York jeweller Harry Schreiner designed some pieces for Christian Dior in the late 1940s and early 1950s. His costume jewellery, worn by such stars as Bette Davis and Marilyn Monroe, is famed for its high-quality diamanté and crystal, and also for its unusual colours, cuts and combinations of paste stones – here imitation turquoise and citrine. Full parures are rare and valuable. In the USA, in the early 1950s, Dior's jewellery was also manufactured by the Kramer company, signed "Christian Dior by Kramer".

Schreiner turquoise and citrine paste brooch, 1960s, diam. 5.5cm/ 2¼in, **£125–150/$190–225**

Floral necklace and earrings in topaz pastes, 1964, necklace l. 42cm/16½in, earrings w. 3.5cm/ 1¼in, **£450–500/$675–750**

▲ Floral necklace & earrings

A necklace and earrings of floral inspiration, by Henkel & Grosse, dated 1964, this set is typical of many versions made in different combinations and colours of pastes through-out the 1950s and 1960s. It shows Dior's skill with iridescent crystals, here in a sparkling mixture of marbleized imitation topaz beads in subtle shades, with simulated baroque pearls and diamanté. Check stones carefully: diamanté or pearls can more easily be replaced than the key coloured pastes, which today are difficult to match exactly.

Large "trembler" diamanté brooch, l. 13cm/5in, 1940s–1950s, **£500–600/ $750–900**

▲ Diamanté lily-of-the-valley "trembler" brooch

Dior's early costume jewellery displays a liking for romantic, graceful pieces in clear diamanté, inspired by 18thC designs. The lily of the valley (*muguet*) is a favourite motif, also interpreted in brooch form by Maison Gripoix for Dior in a gilt-metal and enamel version. This brooch is unsigned, and recent research suggests it was made by the Paris jewellery manufacturer Francis Winter.

1950s glitz

From the early 1950s the costume jewellery industry began to boom all over the world. With the recovery of national economies after World War II and increased spending power, there was renewed interest in novelties, fashion and particularly accessories – the frivolities of everyday living that had to be forgotten during the war. Austrian and Czechoslovakian pastes were once again available, as were base metals suitable for fine settings. In terms of quantity, the USA was the centre of the fashion jewellery trade: in 1955 it was reported that the industry had a turnover of some $180 million a year. Paris, and in particular the "New Look" of Christian Dior (see pp.44-5), often led the way for ideas and colours, but the USA had the ability and technical expertise to translate jewel fashions into glamorous accessories. Dressing up was very much in vogue for the evening; for daywear the subtleties of coloured semi-precious stones became popular.

Corocraft
donkey-and-cart novelty
brooch,
l. 11cm/4¼in,
**£150–200/
$225–300**

▲ Corocraft donkey-and-cart novelty brooch

Coro was the largest manufacturer of costume jewellery in the 1950s, producing a huge range of whimsical novelty brooches with many different themes. This "conversation jewel" is typical of several, probably Hollywood-inspired, that were made with a sentimental Mediterranean or Mexican subject matter.

▼ Weiss necklace & earrings

Albert Weiss, who had worked with Coro, set up his own firm in the 1940s that continued until 1971. He produced high-quality costume jewellery in a wide range of colours and pastes, such as this necklace and earrings in the newly developed "Aurora Borealis" stones (see Fact File opposite). His jewellery is always signed "WEISS", on every piece in a set. In the 1950s he also made jewellery in the Art Deco styles of the 1930s and 1940s.

Weiss necklace
and earrings,
necklace
l. 40.5cm/16in,
earrings
l. 2cm/¾in,
**£100–150/
$150–225**

▼ Weiss flower brooch

Although single
brooches are
generally not the most
collectable 1950s pieces,
there are exceptions such as
the range of floral brooches
by Weiss, which come in
various high-quality pastes
as well as coloured imitation
enamels. Some of these have
matching earrings. Up until a
few years ago these could be
bought for very little, but
recently, as jewels by Weiss
have become increasingly
collectable, prices have risen.

Weiss imitation citrine flower
brooch, late 1950s, l. 8cm/3in,
£40–60/$60–90

Lisner blue necklace and earrings,
necklace l. 43cm/17in, earrings w.
3cm/1¼in, **£100–130/$150–195**

▲ Lisner blue necklace and earrings

As prices for 1950s costume
jewellery by top manufacturers
continue to rise, enthusiasts
for the period discover new
collectable names such as
Lisner. Little is known about
this company, which produced
good-quality, well-designed
costume jewellery in a range
of typical colours and materials.
As with all 1950s costume
jewellery, pieces have to be
in good condition, with no
stones or beads missing
as they are almost
impossible to replace.

▼ Unsigned necklace, bracelet and earrings set

Although signed jewellery
is always the most sought
after, an unsigned set in
an attractive design like
this is still highly desirable
when found complete, with
all the stones intact. This set
may be by a company such
as Lisner, some of whose
pieces are unsigned.

Unsigned necklace, bracelet and
earrings with plastic leaves, 1950s,
necklace l. 43cm/17in, bracelet l.
19cm/7½in, earrings w. 4cm/1½in,
£180–220/$270–330 (the set)

1950s glitz ~ 47

Boucher

Marcel Boucher, one of the most celebrated designers of costume jewellery, began his career in France working as an apprentice model-maker for Cartier. In the 1920s he was transferred from Paris to Cartier's New York workshop. After the 1929 Wall Street crash, the business was cut back and Boucher worked for other jewellers, including Mazer Brothers. In spring 1939 he approached Saks Fifth Avenue with some of his own designs: a group of flamboyant bird brooches, made in coloured rhinestones and bright enamels. These were accepted, went on to become best-sellers, and launched Boucher's career. By 1949 his firm had two offices in New York and a new designer, also French, named Sandra Semensohn. The collaboration proved successful, and they later married. When Boucher died in 1965 Sandra took over the company, which continued to make jewellery until 1970.

▶ **Wheatsheaf brooch**
This is one of Boucher's earliest pieces, of exceptional quality and highly sought after by collectors. He uses pavé-set (snugly fitting) rhinestones, rhodium-plated metal

and exceptional casting to create a piece inspired by romantic turn-of-the-century French originals. It bears the early "MB" mark (used only until the mid-1940s), so small and stylized it is difficult for the untrained eye to make out. The "MB" mark is capped by a Phrygian bonnet, symbol of the French Revolution. Related pieces include a brooch depicting a praying mantis.

Wheatsheaf brooch, late 1930s–40s, l. 11cm/4¼in, **£175–220/$265–330**

▼ **Matching brooch & earrings set**
Although this set dates from the 1950s, its design harks back to the 1940s with its characteristic disc and buckle motifs. As is frequently found in Boucher's pieces, the brooch is signed but not the earrings. This popular design also came with imitation emeralds. Coro produced an almost identical line, but the Coro earrings are signed.

Matching brooch and earrings set, 1950s, brooch diam. 3.5cm/1½in, earrings diam. 2.5cm/1in, **£130–150/$195–225** (the set)

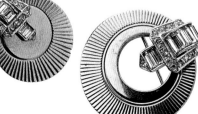

FACT FILE

The model-maker

Boucher's love of mechanics was expressed in some rare jewellery designs, including:
- A "Punchinello" whose arms and legs are raised by pulling on a chain
- A pelican whose beak opens to catch a fish
- A "night and day" series of flowers with petals that open and close.

▼ Poodle brooch

The 1950s saw a craze for the poodle motif, and Boucher designed several appealing versions of a poodle brooch (see also p.5), as well as a popular range of kittens, donkeys, elephants and skunks. Donkeys and elephants sold particularly well at election times: the donkey was a symbol of the Democrat party, and the elephant of the Republicans.

Poodle brooch,
1950s, w. 4.5cm/1¾in,
£60–80/$90–120

Parure, early 1950s, necklace
l. 36cm/14in, bracelet l. 19cm/7½in,
earrings diam. 2.5cm/1in,
£250–300/$375–450

▲ Parure of necklace, bracelet and earrings

Above is a typical Boucher set of the 1950s: chic, "real-looking" design, combining thick gold plate, rhodium plate and rhinestones of different cuts. Boucher was inspired by the revival of the fine jewellery industry in Paris at this time. A complete set such as this is highly collectable, especially as each piece is signed.

▼ Jomaz brooch

Collectors find similarities between 1950s pieces by Boucher and those by Jomaz (previously Joseph Mazer), for whom Boucher had briefly worked. Both designers produced fine pieces based on precious jewellery, using intricate cutting and stone-setting techniques to mount high-quality square-cut or cabochon pastes.

Jomaz brooch, late 1950s,
l. 8cm/3¼in (including pendant),
£150–200/$225–300

Kenneth Jay Lane

Since the 1960s Kenneth Jay Lane has been one of the most successful and popular contemporary designers of costume jewellery. After studying at the Rhode Island School of Design, Lane began working in New York City for *Vogue* magazine, where his work caught the eye of its legendary editor, Diana Vreeland. She loved his bizarre, larger-than-life designs and featured them in the magazine. Lane's career was quickly launched. His designs perfectly matched his often-famous clients' desire for glamour and luxury. Soon Lane began making accessories in his own right, sometimes inspired by precious jewellery, sometimes by the natural world, sometimes by jewels of the past, but always with a keen eye for the needs of the wearer. Jewels by Kenneth Jay Lane have been exhibited in prestigious shows held at the Metropolitan Museum of Art in New York, and there are now many avid collectors of Lane's pieces.

Ali Baba brooch, 1960s, l. 6.5cm/2½in, **£140–160/ $210–240**

▼ Ali Baba brooch
This playful design takes its inspiration from the *Arabian Nights* books and is typical of the sense of fun in jewellery of the 1960s. The piece demonstrates Lane's inventive use of raw materials: here the large high-quality imitation turquoise cabochon used for the belly is of hand-poured French glass with subtle colour variations, of a type not available today. Lane also often used pink and coral glass cabochons in this period. The brooch is signed "K.J.L." on the back, the signature used by Lane until the end of the 1970s. Later, less collectable, pieces are signed "Kenneth Lane" or "Kenneth Jay Lane".

▶ Dragon brooch
The three-dimensional qualities of this highly collectable figural brooch show Lane's innovative use of a range of materials. He mingles gilded base metal, diamanté, black and white enamel, black imitation jet glass and imitation emerald to create a piece that picks up the mythological trends of the 1960s/'70s, while making a witty reference to a classic motif of the Renaissance. The enamel is in mint condition, which is important as chipping or peeling are common and reduce the value significantly.

Dragon brooch, 1960s–1970s, w. 5cm/2in, **£120–140/ $180–210**

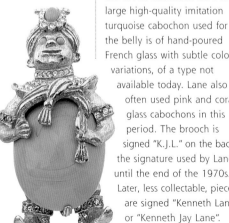

• Complete parures of brooch, earrings, bracelet and necklace are quite rare and highly prized.
• Brooches were often made in several variations.
• "Figural" pins (as opposed to abstract) are highly collectable, particularly in themed groups (such as animals).
• Metal belts of the '60s, typically decorated with fake cabochon stones, are becoming more popular.

▼ Drop earrings

These large-scale glittering earrings would have been made as part of a parure, including a necklace and bracelet or armband, and are in the exotic "Maharajah" mood of the late 1960s/early 1970s. Lane's first designs were based on pieces he saw while in India, and he is still a frequent traveller there today. The earrings below are made of diamanté and plastic pearls, but they convey the extravagance of the genuine materials. They are based on a traditional Indian design, with the central pear-drop shape and fringe of "bobbling" stones. They are signed "K.J.L.".

Pair of large drop earrings, late 1960s/early 1970s, l. 7.5cm/3in, **£130–150/$195–225**

Matching brooch and earrings set, 1960s, brooch w. 9cm/3½in, earrings l. 6cm/2¼in, **£220–260/$330–390**

▲ Matching brooch & earrings set

In Ken Lane's most aristocratic style, this brooch and earrings set was inspired by the designs of Christian Dior, who in his turn harked back to the courtly designs of the 18thC. The set, which would originally have also included a necklace, shows a skilful combination of stones, mingling high-quality imitation topazes of moulded glass, made in Czechoslovakia, with lead crystal jewels of a pale green colour, probably made by Swarovski in imitation of jonquils (semi-precious stones named after the jonquil flower). These stones are difficult to match up if any are missing.

"Big Cat" brooch, 1960s, w. 4.5cm/2in, **£20–30/$30–45**

▲ "Big Cat" brooch

This is one of Lane's series of "Big Cat" jewels, inspired by the designs of Jeanne Toussaint for Cartier and made famous by the Duchess of Windsor. Lane created many versions of these popular panther brooches, in a variety of shapes and materials. Condition is important – the visible wear to the enamel on this piece affects its price considerably. This brooch is also signed "K.J.L.".

The 1960s

"The mood is youth, youth, youth!" wrote the authoritative American publication, *Womens' Wear Daily*. The driving force of the 1960s was innovation and change, fired by youth rebellion, which for the first time in history found a voice and attracted massive publicity. Fashion targeted young people, aided by the ever-increasing availability of inexpensive, mass-produced items. A huge variety of fashion styles overlapped and co-existed, characterized by an unprecedented freedom of design. In this climate of "anything goes", the search for the next big idea was continuous. These ideas were spread and popularized by the growing power of the mass media, through newspapers, magazines and television. In the 1960s the world of fashion and its accessories was obsessed with "image" – as expressed in photography, both moving and still. Costume jewellery became larger, more photogenic, and more conscious of its immediate visual impact.

▶ **Castlecliff Maltese cross**

The 1960s saw a vast range of styles, including updated versions of historical pieces. The Maltese cross, originally made in precious stones for the knights of Malta, became a popular jewel from the Renaissance onwards. In the form of costume jewellery it was produced by Chanel in the 1930s, and again in the 1960s by such leading manufacturers as Ken Lane (see pp.50–51) and Yves Saint Laurent. Here it is interpreted in bold 1960s style by the New York manufacturer, Castlecliff.

Castlecliff Maltese cross, l. 30cm/12in with chain, **£80–90/$120–135**

Selro bracelet and earrings, bracelet l. 18cm/7in, earrings l. 5cm/2in, **£200–230/$300–345**

▼ **Selro bracelet and earrings with oriental head motifs**

Possibly based on Hobé's earlier real-ivory carvings of oriental faces and chessmen, this big, over-the-top 1960s revival of the style is made in plastic and paste. Selro is an American company about which little is known, but it is nevertheless popular with collectors who prize its dramatic, typically 1960s designs. This design is also found in silvered metal with red plastic motifs, as well as on a lariat necklace and brooch.

▼ Coppola e Toppo aqua crystal necklace

Lyda Toppo and Bruno Coppola were a brother-and-sister team who formed Coppola e Toppo in Milan in the late 1940s, producing elaborate costume jewellery in crystal, plastic and Venetian glass beads. In the 1950s they made jewellery for Dior, Balenciaga and Schiaparelli, and in the 1960s for Pucci and Valentino (when Italian fashion became important internationally), as well as under their own name. Early pieces were signed "Miky" (after their dog), but, from the 1950s, "Made in Italy by Coppola & Toppo" appears.

Coppola e Toppo aqua crystal necklace, 1960s, l. 24cm/9½in, **£500–700/$750–1,050**

HAR dragon brooch, 1960s, w. 8cm/3in, **£180–200/$270–300**

▲ HAR dragon brooch

In line with the 1960s' demand for the new and striking, all sorts of unusually coloured metals appeared, such as the green metal used in this dragon brooch by the American manufacturer HAR. Although little is known about the company, its genie, mermaid and dragon theme jewellery commands the highest prices today. This dragon brooch is part of a complete parure that includes necklace, bracelet and earrings. The enamel here is chipped, reducing the value of this piece.

▼ Austrian crystal fruit brooch and earrings

Representing the more traditional side of 1960s costume jewellery, this set of matching fruit brooch and earrings in high-quality frosted crystal has become a hit with collectors. It comes in a variety of fruits, as well as several different and unusual colours. The pieces are all marked "Austria".

Austrian crystal fruit brooch and matching earrings, 1960s, brooch l. 5.5cm/2¼in, earrings l. 3.5cm/1⅜in, **£70–80/$105–120**

Cardin & Space-Age design

In 1961 President Kennedy stood before Congress and said: "I believe this nation should commit itself, before this decade is out, to landing a man on the moon and returning him safely to earth". Throughout the 1960s the idea of space travel gripped the public imagination; designers captured this mood by creating a spare, geometric "Space Age" look, linked to contemporary trends in art. Pierre Cardin, who in 1959 had become the first Paris couturier to open a "ready-to-wear" boutique, and whose innovative designs included a much-publicized outfit for the Beatles, was one of the leaders of this movement. His helmets and cut-outs in dresses and tops called for space-age accessories such as lucite (plastic) and Perspex bangles and rings, necklaces made of huge aluminium discs and geometric earrings that swung and revolved like mobiles. Ironically, by the time Kennedy's vision had become reality in July 1969, the craze for Space-Age styles had mostly given way to the softer, ethnic styles of the hippies.

▼ **Pendant with snakechain**
This pendant is typical of the spare, geometric forms of the Space-Age look developed by Cardin, and would have been used to accessorize the simple "mod" fashions of the early 1960s. Space-Age jewellery rarely employs paste, and is usually of plain metal, plastic or metal and enamel. Snakechains like this appear from the 1920s to the present day: they should be stored gently coiled, or else they can snap irreparably. This item is unsigned; if signed by Cardin or Lanvin it would be worth much more.

Pendant, 1960s, l. 6.5cm/2½in base only, l. 35cm/13¾in with snake-chain, **£50–70/ $75–105**

▶ **Cardin-style pair of plastic earrings**
Earrings were one of the most popular, trend-setting items of Space-Age jewellery, appearing in geometric shapes, squares, circles and psychedelic spirals, and setting off the short, geometric haircuts and bobs devised by the London hairdresser Vidal Sassoon. These earrings echo the shapes of the mobiles designed by Alexander Calder. Colour combinations were intended to shock: green and orange is typical, but most collectable is the black and white of Op Art, as it is considered so characteristic of the period.

Cardin-style pair of plastic earrings, 1960s, l. 7.5cm/3in, **£40–60/ $60–90**

Lucite ring, early 1960s, diam. 4cm/1½in, **£40–60/$60–90**

▲ Lucite ring

The large, chunky rings of the Space-Age style, in plastic and other related materials, were a deliberate contrast to the traditional rings, made in precious stones, of the 1940s and 1950s. Produced in many different bright, rainbow colours, they were fun, novelty items – often several rings would be worn on one hand. Today Space-Age rings are not hugely valuable, but they are a nice collectable of the period. Some of the most sought after are those by Courrèges and Lanvin.

▼ Lucite watch by Pierre Cardin

Space-Age jewellery of the 1960s that is signed "Pierre Cardin" is extremely collectable, particularly when it is in mint condition like this watch. Later Cardin became a ruthless licenser, and his signed pieces from the 1970s and 1980s are much less desirable. Watches are an unusual item of costume jewellery. Check the wind-up mechanism carefully to see if it works, as traditional repairers can be suspicious of unconventional watches. The strap on this watch is PVC, a typical material of the period.

Lucite watch by Pierre Cardin, 1960s, l. 21cm/8¼in, **£400–450/$600–675**

Plastic pendant necklace on snakechain, attributed to Lanvin, early 1970s, l. 35cm/13¾in, **£100–120/$150–180**

▲ Plastic pendant necklace

In the late 1960s the long-established Paris couture house of Lanvin underwent a drastic makeover. A new young designer, Maryl Lanvin, produced a highly collectable series of carved plastic pendants in simple shades of black, ivory, red and green, each hung on chrome-plated chains.

Chanel

For ten years after Coco Chanel's death in 1971, at the age of 88, her company produced collections of clothes, accessories and jewellery that were faithful reissues of her style. In 1983 the brilliant young designer Karl Lagerfeld, who had attended Chanel's first post-war comeback show in 1954, was chosen to direct the house of Chanel, with a brief to reinterpret and modernize. The fashion world waited expectantly: "It was high noon, haute chic and a high point in the fashion calendar of Paris," reported the London *Evening Standard* on 26 January 1983. "The gilt chairs lined up in Chanel's first-floor salon in a narrow street behind the Ritz were labelled Pompidou, Adjani, Rothschild... ." The collection was hailed as a triumph, capturing the spirit of Chanel while ushering in the bold energy of the 1980s, and Lagerfeld's costume jewellery was an essential part of the look. Spurned in the 1990s, this jewellery is now back, and becoming highly collectable.

Gilt-metal rope necklace, 1980s, l. 92cm/36¼in, **£230–280/ $345–420**

▶ **Gilt-metal rope necklace**

Inspired by the sautoirs of Paul Poiret, Coco Chanel introduced long gilt chains in various designs in the early 1930s. The chain is here reinterpreted by Lagerfeld using typical Chanel elements: imitation baroque pearls, gilt coins and "CC" motifs, but in an exaggerated 1980s idiom. The "CC" logo was used discreetly but memorably by Coco Chanel on her signature quilted handbags in the 1950s.

▼ **Pair of large heart-shaped earrings**

Here again, Lagerfeld is drawing on a 1930s design vocabulary, as heart-shaped brooches were made by Chanel in the 1930s. *Pâte-de-verre* was also consistently used, seen in the dark blue centres of these earrings. Dramatic chandelier-type earrings were a favourite accessory in the 1980s, with collectable versions also made by Christian Lacroix.

Pair of large heart-shaped earrings, with *pâte-de-verre*, diamanté and imitation baroque pearl decoration, 1980s, l. 10cm/4in, **£200–220/ $300–330**

▼ Pastel *pâte-de-verre* flower brooch

A reissue of a 1950s style made by Maison Gripoix for Chanel, this brooch is made in a mixture of opaque and translucent *pâte-de-verre*. When held up to the light, it shows tiny air bubbles and sometimes fine cracking, caused while the glass is setting. This does not affect value, whereas chipping does. *Pâte-de-verre* is very fragile and damage is impossible to repair. This 1980s brooch comes in different colours and versions, including a double-headed flower.

Pastel *pâte-de-verre* flower brooch, 1980s, w. 5cm/2in, **£250–300/$375–450**

Three-strand pearl pendant necklace, 1980s, l. 46cm/18in, **£1,000–1,200/$1,500–1,800**

▲ Three-strand pearl pendant necklace

This rare Chanel necklace, made in a limited edition, is a 1980s version of Coco Chanel designs of the 1930s, which she in turn based on Renaissance and baroque precious jewels. It is dated "8" and "2" on the signature plate, meaning 1982. Dating on 1980s Chanel jewellery is not systematic: sometimes it is unnumbered but signed "Chanel Made in France", sometimes it also shows "P" or "A", for *Printemps* and *Automne* (spring and autumn), referring to the relevant collection.

▼ Pair of "CC" earrings

Pictured below is a pair of very collectable earrings showing the "logomania" of the 1980s. Prices are high at the moment for these pieces, leading to much faking; simple gilt logo items are easier to fake than elaborate paste ones. Fakes are lighter in weight and shinier, with signatures less crisp and readable than on the genuine article.

Pair of "CC" earrings, 1980s, l. 6cm/2½in, **£150–200/$225–300**

Collectables of the future

"What will tomorrow's collectable be?" is the question that every lover of costume jewellery asks. Much of it is cheaply made to reflect the passing fads of fashion – worn for a short time, and then thrown away. Better pieces, in terms of design and technique, will probably rise in value over the next few decades and should be kept. As with most future antiques, collectable potential is most often tied to the original sale price, so top-of-the-line items will be the best investment. One certainty is that the potential of costume jewellery as a collectable is increasing all the time. The proliferation of books and specialist periodicals, enthusiasts' conventions and the widely publicized sales of important collections, as well as the new possibilities offered by the internet, ensure that costume jewellery will long continue to give pleasure, and sometimes profit, to the wearer.

▼ **Castlecliff bracelet**
Much costume jewellery of the 1960s was hastily designed, then mass-produced in huge quantities to be sold very cheaply. Those that have stood the test of time are the large, signed pieces that strongly reflect the decade's characteristics, such as this bold cuff bracelet by New York manufacturer Castlecliff, with its good-quality glass stones and textured, satin-finished gilded metal. Castlecliff pieces show an adventurous use of stones, such as black diamanté, imitation jade and lucite.

Castlecliff turquoise bracelet, 1960s, diam. 7.5cm/ 2¾in, **£180–200/ $270–300**

▶ **Large flower brooch by Ian St Gielar**
This highly esteemed American designer, now resident in Florida, was the chief designer for Stanley Hagler (see p.42). After Hagler's death in 1996 he set up on his own. From Hagler, and also Haskell, St Gielar inherits his love of delicate filigree backings on a wide range of brooches, necklaces, bracelets and earrings. Favourite materials include Murano glass (as seen on this brooch), mother-of-pearl, Limoges porcelain and antique ivory. All are in limited editions, always signed on a tag with his name in capital letters.

Large flower brooch by Ian St Gielar, late 1990s, w. 11cm/4¼in, **£170–200/ $255–300**

Large butterfly brooch by Cristobal,
late 1990s, w. 11cm/4¼in,
£90–100/$135–150

▲ Large butterfly brooch by Cristobal

Designers Steve Miners and
Yai, of the London jewellers
Cristobal, use vintage glass
stones from the 1940s and
1950s to create colourful,
eye-catching jewels in limited
editions. Their first design, a
Christmas tree brooch, dates
from the late 1990s and
was an immediate best-seller.
All their pieces are signed
"Cristobal London". Cristobal
pieces have become recent
collectors' items in the UK,
Europe, USA and Japan.

▼ Large cricket brooch by Iradj Moini

With an architect's training,
this Iranian but American-based
jewellery designer started
his career with the fashion
designer Oscar de la Renta.
For the 500th anniversary
celebrations of the Dominican
Republic, organized by de
la Renta, Moini designed
a brightly coloured parrot
brooch, 34cm (13½in) long,
which is now highly sought
after by collectors. The cricket
brooch pictured below is
typical of Moini's inventive,
three-dimensional pieces,
and is one of a series inspired
by the film *A Bug's Life* (1998).

Large cricket brooch by Iradj
Moini, 1990s, l. 13.5cm/5¼in,
£550–600/$825–900

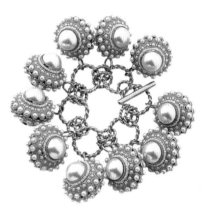

Imitation pearl charm bracelet
by Christian Lacroix,
late 1980s, l. 24cm/9½in,
£175–200/$265–300

▲ Imitation pearl charm bracelet by Christian Lacroix

The couturier Christian Lacroix
(b. 1951) studied art history
before becoming chief
designer to Jean Patou.
In 1987 his first couture
collection celebrated his love
of the folklore in his native
Provence. His bold gypsy
jewellery, including long,
dangling earrings, is becoming
increasingly collectable.

Care & repair

Care and maintenance

When wearing your costume jewellery remember that pieces need careful handling. Always apply hairspray, soap, cream or perfume before you put on jewellery, as cosmetics can damage plated surfaces, imitation pearls, pastes and beads. Before wearing, check that chain links, settings and clasps are secure, as these can weaken over time. Never immerse costume jewellery in water, as this can dissolve adhesive, tarnish metal, discolour paste and shrink or rot string on beaded necklaces and bracelets.

To clean paste stones, spray a cotton bud with a small amount of window-cleaning liquid, squeeze the bud to remove the excess, then gently buff the surface only of each stone. Make sure that the cleaning fluid does not seep into any settings, and pat the jewellery dry with a cotton cloth. To revitalise tired-looking metal settings, use a jeweller's cloth, available from specialist dealers and some hardware or department stores. Avoid polishing creams or dips, and try not to over-polish as patina is desirable on all but the shiniest rhodium finishes.

Store each piece individually in its own box or cloth pochette if possible, but if not wrap it in acid-free paper, available from many antique dealers.

Repair and refurbishment

The most usual hazard for the collector of costume jewellery is the loss of paste stones. A specialist dealer will usually be able to arrange repairs, but they can be costly and slow. Many collectors acquire the simple skills needed to replace missing stones in their costume jewellery, especially if only a small number of replacement stones are required.

The first necessity is a supply of both old and new stones. Some gem wholesalers and lapidaries (craftsmen who cut, polish and set gemstones), as well as art, craft and hobby shops, will stock pastes, marcasites and imitation pearls, and your specialist dealer should be able to put you in touch with the best local sources for these. Many standard colours and cuts are readily available. However, the more unusual shades and shapes can be harder to find, and it is always worth browsing in flea markets and car boot sales for broken bits of jewellery that may match your piece.

To replace lost stones it is best to use clear-drying jeweller's cement, which can be bought through dealers or craft and hobby shops. (For example, a recommended version of this cement is available by post from: H. Marcel Guest Ltd., Riverside Works, Collyhurst Road, Collyhurst, Manchester M40 7RU. Tel: (0161) 205 7631.)

The process is as follows: apply a drop of adhesive onto the end of a safety pin and dab this into the cup-like setting, taking care not to fill it to the edge or the adhesive will spill over. If you see that you have applied too much, a twisted corner of tissue can be used as a wick to absorb excess. A clean cotton cloth should be available for major spills. Never let excess adhesive dry on a stone or setting, as it will be difficult to remove later. Next, pick up your stone, either with your fingers or with tweezers, and push it gently into the setting, then leave it to dry for at least two hours. With prong-set pieces, the prongs have to be carefully opened with a pair of jeweller's pliers and re-closed once the adhesive has dried.

The subject of restoration, and whether it is necessary or advisable, is one on which collectors are divided, and the question of whether or not to restore must ultimately come down to the wearer's preference.

What to read

Here is a selection of books on costume jewellery. Some of them are suitable for those new to the subject, others are more specialist and will be invaluable as your interest develops.

GENERAL
Bennett, David and Mascetti, Daniela
Understanding Jewellery
(Antique Collectors' Club, Woodbridge, 1989)

Culme, John and Rayner, Nicholas
The Jewels of the Duchess of Windsor
(Rizzoli, London, 1987)

Duncan, Alastair
Art Deco (Thames & Hudson, London, 1988)

Giles, Stephen
Miller's Antiques Checklist: Jewellery
(Mitchell Beazley, London, 1997)

Hillier, Bevis
Art Deco of the '20s and '30s
(Schocken, London, 1985)

Menkes, Suzy
The Royal Jewels
(Grafton Pub., London, 1985)

Munn, Geoffrey C.
The Triumph of Love: Jewelry 1530–1930
(Thames & Hudson, London, 1993)

Nadelhoffer, Hans
Cartier: Jewelers Extraordinary
(Thames & Hudson, London, 1984)

Richards, Melissa
Chanel: Key Collections
(Welcome Rain, London, 2000)

Robinson, Julian
Fashion in the Forties
(Academy Editions, London, 1980)

Rudoe, Judy
Cartier 1900–1939
(Harry N. Abrams, London, 1997)

SPECIALIST
Becker, Vivienne
Fabulous Fakes: The History of Fantasy and Fashion Jewellery
(Pavilion Books, London, 1988)

Brunialti, Carla Ginelli
American Costume Jewelry 1935–1950
(Mazzotta, Milan, 1997)

Farneti Cera, Deanna
Costume Jewellery
(Antique Collectors' Club, Woodbridge, 1997)

Farneti Cera, Deanna (et al)
Jewels of Fantasy: Costume Jewelry of the 20th Century
(Harry N. Abrams, New York, 1992)

Farneti Cera, Deanna
The Jewels of Miriam Haskell
(Antique Collectors' Club, Woodbridge, 1997)

Gordon, Angie
Twentieth Century Costume Jewellery
(Adasia Int., London, 1990)

Lancaster, David
Art Nouveau Jewelry (Christie's Collectibles)
(Bulfinch Press, London, 1996)

Miller, Harrice Simons
Costume Jewelry Identification and Price Guide
(Avon Books, New York, 1994)

Moro, Ginger
European Designer Jewelry: A Schiffer Book for Collectors
(Schiffer Publishing, USA, 1995)

Tolkien, Tracy and Wilkinson, Henrietta
A Collector's Guide to Costume Jewelry: Key Styles and How to Recognize Them
(Firefly Books, London, 1997)

PERIODICALS
Vintage Fashion & Costume Jewelry
PO Box 265
Glen Oaks
NY 11004 USA
(published quarterly)

EXHIBITION CATALOGUES
Munn, Geoffrey
One Hundred Tiaras: An Evolution of Style 1800–1990
(Wartski, London, 1997)

Where to buy & see

MAJOR AUCTION HOUSES

Christie's East
219 East 67th Street
New York
New York 10021
USA
Tel: (001) 212 606 0400
Fax: (001) 212 452 2063
www.christies.com

Christie's South Kensington
85 Old Brompton Road
London SW7 3LD UK
Tel: (0044) 20 7581 7611
Fax: (0044) 20 7321 3321

Sotheby's New York
1334 York Avenue
New York
New York 10021
USA
Tel: (001) 212 606 7000
Fax: (001) 212 606 7016
www.sothebys.com

Sotheby's Chicago
215 West Ohio Street
Chicago
Illinois 60610
USA
Tel: (001) 312 396 9599
Fax: (001) 312 396 9598

COSTUME JEWELLERY DEALERS

Beauty and the Beast
Joel Rothman, Unit Q9
Antiquarius Antiques Market
131–141 King's Road
London SW3 8DT UK
Tel: (0044) 20 7351 5149

Cristobal
Stall G125
127 Alfie's Antique Market
13–25 Church Street
London NW8 8DT
UK
Tel: (0044) 20 7724 7789

Steinberg & Tolkien
193 King's Road
London SW3 5EB
UK
Tel: (0044) 20 7376 3660
Fax: (0044) 20 7376 3630

William Wain
Unit J6
Antiquarius Antiques
Market
131–141 King's Road
London SW3 8DT
UK
Tel: (0044) 20 7351 4905

ART NOUVEAU AND ARTS AND CRAFTS JEWELLERY

Kojis
Liberty
214 Regent Street
London W1R 6AH
UK
Tel: (0044) 20 7734 1234
www.liberty.co.uk

Tadema Gallery
10 Charlton Place
Camden Passage
London N1 8AJ
UK
Tel: (0044) 20 7359 1055

MUSEUMS

Birmingham Museum and Art Gallery
Chamberlain Square
Birmingham B3 3DH
UK
Tel: (0044) 121 303 2834
Fax: (0044) 121 303 1394
www.birmingham.gov.uk/bmag

The Metropolitan Museum of Art
1000 Fifth Avenue
New York
New York 10028-0198
USA
Tel: (001) 212 535 7710
www.metmuseum.org

Providence Museum of Jewelry
Flt Cntr Glr
Providence
Rhode Island 02903-000
USA

Victoria & Albert Museum
Cromwell Road
London SW7 2RL
UK
Tel: (0044) 20 7942 2000
www.vam.ac.uk

Index

Acknowledgments

Octopus Publishing Group Ltd/Stuart Chorley: Front and back cover, p2; Butler & Wilson: 1, Butler & Wilson/A.C. Cooper: 7; Octopus Publishing Group Ltd/Steve Tanner/Cristobal: 5t, 6b, 27t, 31b, 32r, 33t, 33bl, 35r, 35b, 37t, 39tl, 39tr, 42c, 42r, 43bl, 45t, 46b, 47t, 47bl, 49t, 49bl, 50l, 50r, 51t, 51bl, 57bl, 58r, 59t; Octopus Publishing Group Ltd/Steve Tanner/William Wain: 6t, 21t, 26b, 29t, 31t, 33br, 37bl, 38t, 40l, 44b, 48b, 53bl; Octopus Publishing Group Ltd/Steve Tanner/Joel Rothman: 8l, 8r, 9t, 9r, 10t, 10b, 11t, 11bl, 11br, 12l, 12r, 13t, 13b, 14l, 14r, 15t, 15bl, 22b, 23t, 23r, 23b, 28r, 59b; Octopus Publishing Group Ltd/Steve Tanner/Steinberg & Tolkien: 9b, 13r, 15br, 20l, 20r, 21b, 22t, 24l, 24r, 25t, 25bl, 25br, 26t, 27t, 27b, 28l, 29bl, 29br, 30t, 30bl, 30br, 31r, 32l, 34l, 34r, 35t, 36l, 36r, 38b, 39br, 40r, 41t, 41r, 41l, 41bl, 42l, 43t, 43r, 44t, 45bl, 46l, 47br, 48t, 49br, 51r, 52t, 52b, 53t, 53br, 54l, 54r, 55tl, 55r, 55b, 56t, 56b, 57t, 57br, 58l, 59r; Tadema Gallery: 16l, 16r, 17tl, 17tr, 17b, 18t, 18b, 19t, 19bl, 19br, 21t; Michael Harvey/Tracy Tolkien: 37br; William Wain: 45r. Key: l = left, r = right, t = top, b = bottom, c = centre. The publishers would like to thank all those who contributed images.